THE REAL INSPECTOR HOUND
AND
AFTER MAGRITTE

The Real Inspector Hound and After Magritte

TWO PLAYS BY
TOM STOPPARD

GROVE PRESS, INC.
NEW YORK

First Evergreen Edition 1975
Second Printing 1977
ISBN: 0-394-17313-9
Grove Press ISBN: 0-8021-0095-3
Library of Congress Catalog Number: 75-995

Manufactured in the United States of America

Distributed by Random House, Inc., New York

GROVE PRESS, INC., 196 West Houston Street,
New York, N.Y. 10014

Contents

THE REAL
INSPECTOR HOUND

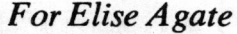

For Elise Agate

The first performance of *The Real Inspector Hound* was given on June 17, 1968, at the Criterion Theatre, London. It was directed by Robert Chetwyn and designed by Hutchinson Scott. The cast was as follows:

MOON	Richard Briers
BIRDBOOT	Ronnie Barker
MRS. DRUDGE	Josephine Tewson
SIMON	Robin Ellis
FELICITY	Patricia Shakesby
CYNTHIA	Caroline Blakiston
MAGNUS	Antony Webb
INSPECTOR HOUND	Hugh Walters

The first thing is that the audience appear to be confronted by their own reflection in a huge mirror. Impossible. However, back there in the gloom—not at the footlights—a bank of plush seats and pale smudges of faces. The total effect having been established, it can be progressively faded out as the play goes on, until the front row remains to remind us of the rest and then, finally, merely two seats in that row—one of which is now occupied by MOON. *Between* MOON *and the auditorium is an acting area which represents, in as realistic an idiom as possible, the drawing-room of Muldoon Manor. French windows at one side. A telephone fairly well upstage (i.e. towards* MOON*). The body of a man lies sprawled face down on the floor in front of a large settee. This settee must be of a size and design to allow it to be wheeled over the body, hiding it completely. Silence. The room. The body.* MOON.

MOON *stares blankly ahead. He turns his head to one side then the other, then up, then down—waiting. He picks up his programme and reads the front cover. He turns over the page and reads.*

He turns over the page and reads.

He turns over the page and reads.

He turns over the page and reads.

He looks at the back cover and reads.

He puts it down, crosses his legs, and looks about. He stares front. Behind him and to one side, barely visible, a man enters and sits down: BIRDBOOT.

7

Pause. MOON *picks up his programme, glances at the front cover and puts it down impatiently. Pause. . . . Behind him there is the crackle of a chocolate-box, absurdly loud.* MOON *looks round. He and* BIRDBOOT *see each other. They are clearly known to each other. They acknowledge each other with constrained waves.* MOON *looks straight ahead.* BIRDBOOT *comes down to join him.*

Note: Almost always, MOON *and* BIRDBOOT *converse in tones suitable for an auditorium, sometimes a whisper. However good the acoustics might be, they will have to have microphones where they are sitting. The effect must be not of sound picked up, amplified and flung out at the audience, but of sound picked up, carried and gently dispersed around the auditorium.*

Anyway, BIRDBOOT, *with a box of Black Magic chocolates, makes his way down to join* MOON *and plumps himself down next to him, plumpish, middle-aged* BIRDBOOT *and younger, taller, less-relaxed* MOON.

BIRDBOOT (*sitting down; conspiratorially*): Me and the lads have had a meeting in the bar and decided it's first-class family entertainment but if it goes on beyond half-past ten it's self-indulgent—pass it on . . . (*and laughs jovially.*) I'm on my own tonight, don't mind if I join you?

MOON: Hello, Birdboot.

BIRDBOOT: Where's Higgs?

MOON: I'm standing in.

MOON *and* BIRDBOOT: Where's Higgs?

MOON: Every time.

BIRDBOOT: What?

8

MOON: It is as if we only existed one at a time, combining to achieve continuity. I keep space warm for Higgs. My presence defines his absence, his absence confirms my presence, his presence precludes mine. . . . When Higgs and I walk down this aisle together to claim our common seat, the oceans will fall into the sky and the trees will hang with fishes.

BIRDBOOT (*he has not been paying attention, looking around vaguely, now catches up*): Where's Higgs?

MOON: The very sight of me with a complimentary ticket is enough. The streets are impassable tonight, the country is rising and the cry goes up from hill to hill—Where—is—Higgs? (*Small pause.*) Perhaps he's dead at last, or trapped in a lift somewhere, or succumbed to amnesia, wandering the land with his turn-ups stuffed with ticket-stubs.

BIRDBOOT *regards him doubtfully for a moment.*

BIRDBOOT: Yes . . . Yes, well I didn't bring Myrtle tonight—not exactly her cup of tea, I thought, tonight.

MOON: Over her head, you mean?

BIRDBOOT: Well, no—I mean it's a sort of a *thriller*, isn't it?

MOON: Is it?

BIRDBOOT: That's what I heard. Who-killed thing?—no-one-will-leave-the-house?

MOON: I suppose so. Underneath.

BIRDBOOT: *Underneath?!?* It's a whodunnit, man!—Look at it!

They look at it. The room. The body. Silence.

Has it started yet?

9

MOON: Yes.

Pause. They look at it.

BIRDBOOT: Are you sure?

MOON: It's a pause.

BIRDBOOT: You can't start with a *pause!* If you want my opinion there's total panic back there. (*Laughs and subsides.*) Where's Higgs tonight, then?

MOON: It will follow me to the grave and become my epitaph—Here lies Moon the second string: where's Higgs? . . . Sometimes I dream of revolution, a bloody *coup d'état* by the second rank—troupes of actors slaughtered by their understudies, magicians sawn in half by indefatigably smiling glamour girls, cricket teams wiped out by marauding bands of twelfth men—I dream of champions chopped down by rabbit-punching sparring partners while eternal bridesmaids turn and rape the bridegrooms over the sausage rolls and parliamentary private secretaries plant bombs in the Minister's Humber—comedians die on provincial stages, robbed of their feeds by mutely triumphant stooges—And march—an army of assistants and deputies, the seconds-in-command, the runners-up, the right-hand men—storming the palace gates wherein the second son has already mounted the throne having committed regicide with a croquet mallet—stand-ins of the world stand up!—

Beat.

Sometimes I dream of Higgs.

Pause. BIRDBOOT *regards him doubtfully. He is at a loss, and grasps reality in the form of his box of chocolates.*

BIRDBOOT (*chewing into mike*): Have a chocolate!

MOON: What kind?

BIRDBOOT (*chewing into mike*): Black Magic.

MOON: No thanks.

> *Chewing stops dead.*
> *Of such tiny victories and defeats . . .*

BIRDBOOT: I'll give you a tip, then. Watch the girl.

MOON: You think she did it?

BIRDBOOT: No, no—the *girl*, watch her.

MOON: What girl?

BIRDBOOT: You won't know her. I'll give you a nudge.

MOON: *You* know her, do you?

BIRDBOOT (*suspiciously, bridling*): What's *that* supposed to mean?

MOON: I beg your pardon?

BIRDBOOT: I'm trying to tip you a wink—give you a nudge as good as a tip—for God's sake, Moon, what's the matter with you?—you could do yourself some good, spotting her first time out—she's new, from the provinces, going straight to the top. I don't want to put words into your mouth but a word from us and we could make her.

MOON: I suppose you've made dozens of them, like that.

BIRDBOOT (*instantly outraged*): I'll have you know I'm a family man devoted to my homely but good-natured wife, and if you're suggesting—

MOON: No, no—

BIRDBOOT: —A man of my scrupulous morality—

MOON: I'm sorry—

BIRDBOOT: —falsely besmirched—

MOON: Is that her?

> *For* MRS. DRUDGE *has entered.*

BIRDBOOT: —don't be absurd, wouldn't be seen dead with the old—ah.

MRS. DRUDGE *is the char, middle-aged, turbanned. She heads straight for the radio, dusting on the trot.*

MOON (*reading his programme*): Mrs. Drudge the Help.

RADIO (*without preamble, having been switched on by* MRS. DRUDGE): We interrupt our programme for a special police message.

MRS. DRUDGE *stops to listen.*

The search still goes on for the escaped madman who is on the run in Essex.

MRS. DRUDGE (*fear and dismay*): Essex!

RADIO: County police led by Inspector Hound have received a report that the man has been seen in the desolate marshes around Muldoon Manor.

Fearful gasp from MRS. DRUDGE.

The man is wearing a darkish suit with a lightish shirt. He is of medium height and build and youngish. Anyone seeing a man answering to this description and acting suspiciously, is advised to phone the nearest police station.

A man answering this description has appeared behind MRS. DRUDGE. *He is acting suspiciously. He creeps in. He creeps out.* MRS. DRUDGE *does not see him. He does not see the body.*

That is the end of the police message.

MRS. DRUDGE *turns off the radio and resumes her cleaning. She does not see the body. Quite fortuitously, her view of the body is always blocked, and when it isn't she has her back to it. However, she is dusting and polishing her way towards it.*

BIRDBOOT: So that's what they say about me, is it?

MOON: What?

BIRDBOOT: Oh, I know what goes on behind my back—sniggers—slanders—hole-in-corner innuendo—What have you heard?

MOON: Nothing.

BIRDBOOT (*urbanely*): Tittle tattle. Tittle, my dear fellow, tattle. I take no notice of it—the sly envy of scandal mongers—I can afford to ignore them, I'm a respectable married man—

MOON: Incidentally—

BIRDBOOT: Water off a duck's back, I assure you.

MOON: Who was that lady I saw you with last night?

BIRDBOOT (*unexpectedly stung into fury*): How dare you! (*More quietly.*) How dare you. Don't you come here with your slimy insinuations! My wife Myrtle understands perfectly well that a man of my critical standing is obliged occasionally to mingle with the world of the footlights, simply by way of keeping *au fait* with the latest—

MOON: I'm sorry—

BIRDBOOT: That a critic of my scrupulous integrity should be vilified and pilloried in the stocks of common gossip—

MOON: Sssh—

BIRDBOOT: I have nothing to hide!—why, if this should reach the ears of my beloved Myrtle—

MOON: Can I have a chocolate?

BIRDBOOT: What? Oh—(*Mollified.*) Oh yes—my dear fellow—yes, let's have a chocolate—No point in—yes, good show. (*Pops chocolate into his mouth and chews.*) Which one do you fancy?—Cherry? Strawberry? Coffee cream? Turkish delight?

MOON: I'll have montelimar.

Chewing stops.

BIRDBOOT: Ah. Sorry. (*Just missed that one.*)

MOON: Gooseberry fondue?

BIRDBOOT: No.

MOON: Pistacchio fudge? Nectarine cluster? Hickory nut praline? Château Neuf du Pape '55 cracknell?

BIRDBOOT: I'm afraid not. . . . Caramel?

MOON: Yes, all right.

BIRDBOOT: Thanks very much. (*He gives* MOON *a chocolate. Pause.*) Incidentally, old chap, I'd be grateful if you didn't mention—I mean, you know how these misunderstandings get about. . . .

MOON: What?

BIRDBOOT: The fact is, Myrtle simply doesn't *like* the theatre . . . (*He trails off hopelessly.*)

MRS. DRUDGE, *whose discovery of the body has been imminent, now—by way of tidying the room —slides the couch over the corpse, hiding it completely. She resumes dusting and humming.*

MOON: By the way, congratulations, Birdboot.

BIRDBOOT: What?

MOON: At the Theatre Royal. Your entire review reproduced in neon!

BIRDBOOT (*pleased*): Oh . . . that old thing.

MOON: You've seen it, of course.

BIRDBOOT (*vaguely*): Well, I was passing. . . .

MOON: I definitely intend to take a second look when it has settled down.

BIRDBOOT: As a matter of fact I have a few colour transparencies—I don't know whether you'd care to . . ?

MOON: Please, please—love to, love to . . .

BIRDBOOT hands over a few colour slides and a battery-powered viewer which MOON holds up to his eyes as he speaks.

Yes . . . yes . . . lovely . . . awfully sound. It has scale, it has colour, it is, in the best sense of the word, electric. Large as it is, it is a small masterpiece—I would go so far as to say—kinetic without being pop, and having said that, I think it must be said that here we have a review that adds a new dimension to the critical scene. I urge you to make haste to the Theatre Royal, for this is the stuff of life itself. (*Handing back the slides, morosely.*) All I ever got was "Unforgettable" on the posters for . . . What was it?

BIRDBOOT: Oh—yes— I know . . . Was that you? I thought it was Higgs.

The phone rings. MRS. DRUDGE seems to have been waiting for it to do so and for the last few seconds has been dusting it with an intense concentration. She snatches it up.

MRS. DRUDGE (*into phone*): Hello, the drawing-room of Lady Muldoon's country residence one morning in early spring? . . . He*llo!*—the draw—Who? Whom did you wish to speak to? I'm afraid there is no one of that name here, this is all very mysterious and I'm sure it's leading up to something, I hope nothing is amiss for we, that is Lady Muldoon and her houseguests, are here cut off from the world, including Magnus, the wheelchair-ridden half-brother of her ladyship's husband Lord Albert Muldoon who ten years ago went out for a walk on the cliffs and was never seen again.

MOON: Derivative, of course.

BIRDBOOT: But quite sound.

MRS. DRUDGE: Should a stranger enter our midst, which I very much doubt, I will tell him you called. Good-bye.

She puts down the phone and catches sight of the previously seen suspicious character who has now entered again, more suspiciously than ever, through the French windows. He senses her stare, freezes, and straightens up.

SIMON: Ah!—hello there! I'm Simon Gascoyne, I hope you don't mind, the door was open so I wandered in. I'm a friend of Lady Muldoon, the lady of the house, having made her acquaintance through a mutual friend, Felicity Cunningham, shortly after moving into this neighbourhood just the other day.

MRS. DRUDGE: I'm Mrs. Drudge. I don't live in but I pop in on my bicycle when the weather allows to help in the running of charming though somewhat isolated Muldoon Manor. Judging by the time (*she glances at the clock*) you did well to get here before high water cut us off for all practical purposes from the outside world.

SIMON: I took the short cut over the cliffs and followed

one of the old smugglers' paths through the treacherous swamps that surround this strangely inaccessible house.

MRS. DRUDGE: Yes, many visitors have remarked on the topographical quirk in the local strata whereby there are no roads leading from the Manor, though there *are* ways of getting *to* it, weather allowing.

SIMON: Yes, well I must say it's a lovely day so far.

MRS. DRUDGE: Ah, but now that the cuckoo-beard is in bud there'll be fog before the sun hits Foster's Ridge.

SIMON: I say, it's wonderful how you country people really know weather.

MRS. DRUDGE (*suspiciously*): Know whether what?

SIMON (*glancing out of the window*): Yes, it does seem to be coming on a bit foggy.

MRS. DRUDGE: The fog is very treacherous around here— it rolls off the sea without warning, shrouding the cliffs in a deadly mantle of blind man's buff.

SIMON: Yes, I've heard it said.

MRS. DRUDGE: I've known whole week-ends when Muldoon Manor, as this lovely old Queen Anne House is called, might as well have been floating on the pack ice for all the good it would have done phoning the police. It was on such a week-end as this that Lord Muldoon who had lately brought his beautiful bride back to the home of his ancestors, walked out of this house ten years ago, and his body was never found.

SIMON: Yes indeed, poor Cynthia.

MRS. DRUDGE: His name was Albert.

SIMON: Yes indeed, poor Albert. But tell me, is Lady Muldoon about?

MRS. DRUDGE: I believe she is playing tennis on the lawn with Felicity Cunningham.

SIMON (*startled*): Felicity Cunningham?

MRS. DRUDGE: A mutual friend, I believe you said. A happy chance. I will tell them you are here.

SIMON: Well, I can't really stay as a matter of fact—please don't disturb them—I really should be off.

MRS. DRUDGE: They would be very disappointed. It is some time since we have had a four for pontoon bridge at the Manor, and I don't play cards myself.

SIMON: There is another guest, then?

MRS. DRUDGE: Major Magnus, the crippled half-brother of Lord Muldoon who turned up out of the blue from Canada just the other day, completes the house-party.

MRS. DRUDGE *leaves on this.* SIMON *is undecided.*

MOON (*ruminating quietly*): I think I must be waiting for Higgs to die.

BIRDBOOT: What?

MOON: Half-afraid that I will vanish when he does.

The phone rings. SIMON *picks it up.*

SIMON: Hello?

MOON: I wonder if it's the same for Puckeridge?

BIRDBOOT *and* SIMON (*together*): Who?

MOON: Third string.

BIRDBOOT: Your stand-in?

MOON: Does he wait for Higgs and I to write each other's obituary—does he dream—?

SIMON: To whom did you wish to speak?

BIRDBOOT: What's he like?

MOON: Bitter.

SIMON: There is no one of that name here.

BIRDBOOT: No—as a critic, what's Puckeridge like as a critic?

MOON (*laughs poisonously*): Nobody knows—

SIMON: You must have got the wrong number!

MOON: —There's always been me and Higgs.

SIMON *replaces the phone and paces nervously. Pause.* BIRDBOOT *consults his programme.*

BIRDBOOT: Simon Gascoyne. It's not him, of course.

MOON: What?

BIRDBOOT: I said it's not him.

MOON: Who is it, then?

BIRDBOOT: My guess is Magnus.

MOON: In disguise, you mean?

BIRDBOOT: What?

MOON: You think he's Magnus in disguise?

BIRDBOOT: I don't think you're concentrating, Moon.

MOON: I thought you said—

BIRDBOOT: You keep chattering on about Higgs and Puckeridge—what's the matter with you?

MOON (*thoughtfully*): I wonder if they talk about me . . . ?

A strange impulse makes SIMON *turn on the radio.*

RADIO: Here is another police message. Essex County police are still searching in vain for the madman who is at large in the deadly marshes of the coastal region. Inspector Hound who is masterminding the operation, is not available for comment but it is widely believed that he has a secret plan. . . . Meanwhile police and volunteers are combing the swamps with loud-hailers, shouting, "Don't be a madman, give yourself up." That is the end of the police message.

SIMON *turns off the radio. He is clearly nervous.* MOON *and* BIRDBOOT *are on separate tracks.*

BIRDBOOT (*knowingly*): Oh yes . . .

MOON: Yes, I should think my name is seldom off Puckeridge's lips . . . sad, really. I mean, it's no life at all, a stand-in's stand-in.

BIRDBOOT: Yes . . . yes . . .

MOON: Higgs never gives me a second thought. I can tell by the way he nods.

BIRDBOOT: Revenge, of course.

MOON: What?

BIRDBOOT: Jealousy.

MOON: Nonsense—there's nothing *personal* in it—

BIRDBOOT: The paranoid grudge—

MOON (*sharply first, then starting to career . . .*): It is merely that it is not enough to wax at another's wane, to be held in reserve, to be on hand, on call, to step in or not at all, the substitute—the near offer —the temporary-acting—for I am Moon, continuous Moon, in my own shoes, Moon in June, April, September and no member of the human race keeps warm my bit of space—yes, I can tell by the way he nods.

BIRDBOOT: Quite mad, of course.

MOON: What?

BIRDBOOT: The answer lies out there in the swamps.

MOON: Oh.

BIRDBOOT: The skeleton in the cupboard is coming home to roost.

MOON: Oh yes. (*He clears his throat . . . for both he and*

20

BIRDBOOT *have a "public" voice, a critic voice which they turn on for sustained pronouncements of opinion.*) Already in the opening stages we note the classic impact of the catalystic figure—the outsider —plunging through to the centre of an ordered world and setting up the disruptions—the shock waves—which unless I am much mistaken, will strip these comfortable people—these crustaceans in the rock pool of society—strip them of their shells and leave them exposed as the trembling raw meat which, at heart, is all of us. But there is more to it than that—

BIRDBOOT: I agree—keep your eye on Magnus.

A tennis ball bounces through the French windows, closely followed by FELICITY, *who is in her twenties. She wears a pretty tennis outfit, and carries a racket.*

FELICITY (*calling behind her*): Out!

It takes her a moment to notice SIMON *who is standing shiftily to one side.* MOON *is stirred by a memory.*

MOON: I say, Birdboot . . .
BIRDBOOT: That's the one.
FELICITY (*catching sight of* SIMON): You!

Felicity's manner at the moment is one of great surprise but some pleasure.

SIMON (*nervously*): Er, yes—hello again.
FELICITY: What are you doing here?
SIMON: Well, I . . .

MOON: She's—

BIRDBOOT: Sssh . . .

SIMON: No doubt you're surprised to see me.

FELICITY: Honestly, darling, you really are extraordinary.

SIMON: Yes, well, here I am.

FELICITY: You must have been desperate to see me—I mean, I'm *flattered*, but couldn't it wait till I got back?

SIMON (*bravely*): There is something you don't know.

FELICITY: What is it?

SIMON: Look, about the things I said—it may be that I got carried away a little—we both did—

FELICITY (*stiffly*): What are you trying to say?

SIMON: I love another!

FELICITY: I see.

SIMON: I didn't make any promises—I merely—

FELICITY: You don't have to say any more—

SIMON: Oh, I didn't want to hurt you—

FELICITY: Of all the nerve!

SIMON: Well, I—

FELICITY: You philandering coward—

SIMON: Let me explain—

FELICITY: This is hardly the time and place—you think you can barge in anywhere, whatever I happen to be doing—

SIMON: But I want you to know that my admiration for you is sincere—I don't want you to think that I didn't mean those things I said—

FELICITY: I'll kill you for this, Simon Gascoyne!

She leaves in tears, passing MRS. DRUDGE *who has entered in time to overhear her last remark.*

MOON: It was her.

BIRDBOOT: I told you—straight to the top—

MOON: No, no—

BIRDBOOT: Sssh. . . .

SIMON (*to* MRS. DRUDGE): Yes, what is it?

MRS. DRUDGE: I have come to set up the card table, sir.

SIMON: I don't think I can stay.

MRS. DRUDGE: Oh, Lady Muldoon *will* be disappointed.

SIMON: Does she know I'm here?

MRS. DRUDGE: Oh yes, sir, I just told her and it put her in quite a tizzy.

SIMON: Really? . . . Well, I suppose now that I've cleared the air . . . Quite a tizzy, you say . . . really . . . really . . .

He and MRS. DRUDGE *start setting up for card game.* MRS. DRUDGE *leaves when this is done.*

MOON: Felicity!—she's the one.

BIRDBOOT: Nonsense—red herring.

MOON: I mean, it was *her!*

BIRDBOOT (*exasperated*): *What* was?

MOON: That lady I saw you with last night!

BIRDBOOT (*inhales with fury*): Are you suggesting that a man of my scrupulous integrity would trade his pen for a mess of pottage?! Simply because in the course of my profession I happen to have struck up an acquaintance—to have, that is, a warm regard, if you like, for a fellow toiler in the vineyard of greasepaint—I find it simply intolerable to be pillified and viloried—

MOON: I never implied—

BIRDBOOT: —to find myself the object of uninformed malice, the petty slanders of little men—

23

MOON: I'm sorry—

BIRDBOOT: —to suggest that my good opinion in a journal of unimpeachable integrity is at the disposal of the first coquette who gives me what I want—

MOON: Sssssh—

BIRDBOOT: A ladies' man! . . . Why, Myrtle and I have been together now for—Christ!—who's *that?*

Enter LADY CYNTHIA MULDOON *through French windows. A beautiful woman in her thirties. She wears a cocktail dress, is formally coiffured, and carries a tennis racket.*

Her effect on BIRDBOOT *is also impressive. He half-rises and sinks back agape.*

CYNTHIA (*entering*): Simon!

A dramatic freeze between her and SIMON.

MOON: Lady Muldoon.

BIRDBOOT: No, I mean—who *is* she?

SIMON (*coming forward*): Cynthia!

CYNTHIA: Don't say anything for a moment—just hold me.

He seizes her and glues his lips to hers, as they say. While their lips are glued—

BIRDBOOT: She's *beautiful*—a vision of eternal grace, a poem . . .

MOON: I think she's got her mouth open.

CYNTHIA *breaks away dramatically.*

CYNTHIA: We can't go on meeting like this!

SIMON: We have nothing to be ashamed of!

CYNTHIA: But darling, this is madness!

SIMON: Yes!—I am mad with love for you!

CYNTHIA: Please—remember where we are!

SIMON: Cynthia, I love you!

CYNTHIA: Don't—I love Albert!

SIMON: He's dead! (*Shaking her.*) Do you understand me—Albert's dead!

CYNTHIA: No—I'll never give up hope! Let me go! We are not free!

SIMON: I don't care, we were meant for each other—had we but met in time.

CYNTHIA: You're a cad, Simon! You will use me and cast me aside as you have cast aside so many others.

SIMON: No, Cynthia!—you can make me a better person!

CYNTHIA: You're ruthless—so strong, so cruel—

Ruthlessly he kisses her.

MOON: The son she never had, now projected in this handsome stranger and transformed into lover—youth, vigour, the animal, the athlete as aesthete —breaking down the barriers at the deepest level of desire.

BIRDBOOT: By jove, I think you're right. Her mouth *is* open.

CYNTHIA *breaks away.* MRS. DRUDGE *has entered.*

CYNTHIA: Stop—can't you see you're making a fool of yourself!

SIMON: I'll kill anyone who comes between us!

CYNTHIA: Yes, what is it, Mrs. Drudge?

MRS. DRUDGE: Should I close the windows, my lady? The fog is beginning to roll off the sea like a deadly—

CYNTHIA: Yes, you'd better. It looks as if we're in for one of those days. Are the cards ready?

MRS. DRUDGE: Yes, my lady.

CYNTHIA: Would you tell Miss Cunningham we are waiting.

MRS. DRUDGE: Yes, my lady.

CYNTHIA: And fetch the Major down.

MRS. DRUDGE (*as she leaves*): I think I hear him coming downstairs now.

She does: the sound of a wheelchair approaching down several flights of stairs with landings in between. It arrives bearing MAGNUS *at about 15 m.p.h., knocking* SIMON *over violently.*

CYNTHIA: Simon!

MAGNUS (*roaring*): Never had a chance! Ran under the wheels!

CYNTHIA: Darling, are you all right?

MAGNUS: I have witnesses!

CYNTHIA: Oh, Simon—say something!

SIMON (*sitting up suddenly*): I'm most frightfully sorry.

MAGNUS (*still shouting*): How long have you been a pedestrian?

SIMON: Ever since I could walk.

CYNTHIA: Can you walk now . . . ?

SIMON *rises and walks.*

Thank God! Magnus, this is Simon Gascoyne.

MAGNUS: What's he doing here?

CYNTHIA: He just turned up.

MAGNUS: Really? How do you like it here?

SIMON (*to* CYNTHIA): I could stay forever.

FELICITY *enters.*

FELICITY: So— You're still here.

CYNTHIA: Of course he's still here. We're going to play cards. There's no need to introduce you two, is there, for I recall now that you, Simon, met me through Felicity, our mutual friend.

FELICITY: Yes, Simon is an old friend, though not as old as you, Cynthia dear.

SIMON: Yes, I haven't seen Felicity since—

FELICITY: Last night.

CYNTHIA: Indeed? Well, you deal, Felicity. Simon, you help me with the sofa. Will you partner Felicity, Magnus, against Simon and me?

MAGNUS (*aside*): Will Simon and you always be partnered against me, Cynthia?

CYNTHIA: What do you mean, Magnus?

MAGNUS: You are a damned attractive woman, Cynthia.

CYNTHIA: Please! Please! Remember Albert!

MAGNUS: Albert's dead, Cynthia—and you are still young. I'm sure he would have wished that you and I—

CYNTHIA: No, Magnus, this is not to be!

MAGNUS: It's Gascoyne, isn't it? I'll kill him if he comes between us.

CYNTHIA (*calling*): Simon!

The sofa is shoved towards the card table, once more revealing the corpse, though not to the players.

BIRDBOOT: Simon's for the chop all right.

CYNTHIA: Right! Who starts?

MAGNUS: I do. No bid.

They start playing, putting down and picking up cards.

CYNTHIA: Did I hear you say you saw Felicity last night, Simon?

SIMON; Did I?—Ah yes, yes quite—your turn, Felicity.

FELICITY: I've had my turn, haven't I, Simon?—now, it seems, it's Cynthia's turn.

CYNTHIA; That's my trick, Felicity dear.

FELICITY: Hell hath no fury like a woman scorned, Simon.

SIMON: Yes, I've heard it said.

FELICITY: So I hope you have not been cheating, Simon.

SIMON (*standing up and throwing down his cards*): No, Felicity, it's just that I hold the cards!

CYNTHIA: Well done, Simon!

MAGNUS *pays* SIMON *generously in blank notes, while* CYNTHIA *deals.*

FELICITY: Strange how Simon appeared in the neighbourhood from nowhere. We know so little about him.

SIMON: It doesn't always pay to show your hand!

CYNTHIA: Right! Simon, it's your opening on the minor bid.

SIMON *plays.*

CYNTHIA: Hm, let's see. . . . (*Plays.*)

FELICITY: I hear there's a dangerous madman on the loose.

CYNTHIA: Simon?

SIMON: Yes—yes—sorry. (*Plays.*)

CYNTHIA: I meld.

FELICITY: Yes—personally, I think he's been hiding out in the deserted cottage on the cliffs (*plays*).

SIMON: Flush!

CYNTHIA: No! Simon—your luck's in tonight!

FELICITY: We shall see—the night is not over yet, Simon Gascoyne! (*She exits.*)

Once more MAGNUS *pays* SIMON.

SIMON (*to* MAGNUS): So you're the crippled half-brother of Lord Muldoon who turned up out of the blue from Canada just the other day, are you? It's taken you a long time to get here. What did you do—walk? Oh, I say, I'm most frightfully sorry!

MAGNUS: Care for a spin round the rose garden, Cynthia?

CYNTHIA: No Magnus, I must talk to Simon.

SIMON: My round, I think, Major.

MAGNUS: You think so?

SIMON: Yes, Major—I do.

MAGNUS: There's an old Canadian proverb handed down from the Blackfoot Indians, which says: He who laughs last laughs longest.

SIMON: Yes, I've heard it said.

CYNTHIA (*calling*): Simon!

MAGNUS: Well, I think I'll go and oil my gun. (*He exits.*)

CYNTHIA: I think Magnus suspects something. And Felicity . . . Simon, was there anything between you and Felicity?

SIMON: No, no—it's over between her and me, Cynthia—it was a mere passing fleeting thing we had—but now that I have found you—

CYNTHIA: If I find that you have been untrue to me—if I find that you have falsely seduced me from my dear husband Albert—I will kill you, Simon Gascoyne!

MRS. DRUDGE *has entered silently to witness this. On this tableau, pregnant with significance, the act ends, the body still undiscovered. Perfunctory applause.*

MOON *and* BIRDBOOT *seem to be completely preoccupied, becoming audible, as it were.*

MOON: Camps it around the Old Vic in his opera cloak and passes me the tat.

BIRDBOOT: Do you believe in love at first sight?

MOON: It's not that I think I'm a better critic—

BIRDBOOT: I feel my whole life changing—

MOON: I am but it's not that.

BIRDBOOT: Oh, the world will laugh at me, I know . . .

MOON: It is not that they are much in the way of shoes to step into . . .

BIRDBOOT: . . . call me an infatuated old fool . . .

MOON: . . . They are not.

BIRDBOOT: . . . condemn me . . .

MOON: He is standing in my light, that is all.

BIRDBOOT: . . . betrayer of my class . . .

MOON: . . . an almost continuous eclipse, interrupted by the phenomenon of moonlight.

BIRDBOOT: I don't care, I'm a goner.

MOON: And I dream . . .

BIRDBOOT: The Blue Angel all over again.

MOON: . . . of the day his temperature climbs through the top of his head . . .

BIRDBOOT: Ah, the sweet madness of love . . .

MOON: . . . of the spasm on the stairs . . .

BIRDBOOT: Myrtle, farewell . . .

MOON: . . . dreaming of the stair he'll never reach—

BIRDBOOT: —for I only live but once. . . .

MOON: Sometimes I dream that I've killed him.

BIRDBOOT: What?

MOON: What?

They pull themselves together.

BIRDBOOT: Yes . . . yes. . . . A beautiful performance, a collector's piece. I shall say so.

MOON: A very promising debut. I'll put in a good word.

BIRDBOOT: It would be as hypocritical of me to withhold praise on grounds of personal feelings, as to withhold censure.

MOON: You're right. Courageous.

BIRDBOOT: Oh, I know what people will say— There goes Birdboot buttering up his latest—

MOON: Ignore them—

BIRDBOOT: But I rise above that— The fact is I genuinely believe her performance to be one of the summits in the range of contemporary theatre.

MOON: Trim-buttocked, that's the word for her.

BIRDBOOT: —the radiance, the inner sadness—

MOON: Does she actually come across with it?

BIRDBOOT: The part as written is a mere cypher but she manages to make Cynthia a real person—

MOON: *Cynthia?*

BIRDBOOT: And should she, as a result, care to meet me over a drink, simply by way of er—thanking me, as it were—

MOON: Well, you fickle old bastard!

BIRDBOOT (*aggressively*): Are you suggesting . . . ? (*He shudders to a halt and clears his throat.*) Well now—shaping up quite nicely, wouldn't you say?

MOON: Oh yes, yes. A nice trichotomy of forces. One must reserve judgement of course, until the confrontation, but I think it's pretty clear where we're heading.

BIRDBOOT: I agree. It's Magnus a mile off.

Small pause.

MOON: What's Magnus a mile off?

BIRDBOOT: If we knew that we wouldn't be here.

MOON (*clears throat*): Let me at once say that it has *élan* while at the same time avoiding *éclat*. Having said that, and I think it must be said, I am bound to ask—does this play know where it is going?

BIRDBOOT: Well, it seems open and shut to me, Moon— Magnus is not what he pretends to be and he's got his next victim marked down—

MOON: Does it, I repeat, declare its affiliations? There are moments, and I would not begrudge it this, when the play, if we can call it that, and I think on balance we can, aligns itself uncompromisingly on the side of life. *Je suis*, it seems to be saying, *ergo sum.* But is that enough? I think we are entitled to ask. For what in fact is this play concerned with? It is my belief that here we are concerned with what I have referred to elsewhere as the nature of identity. I think we are entitled to ask—and here one is irresistibly reminded of Voltaire's cry, "*Voilà*"—I think we are entitled to ask— *Where is God?*

BIRDBOOT (*stunned*): Who?

MOON: Go-od.

BIRDBOOT (*peeping furtively into his programme*): God?

MOON: I think we are entitled to ask.

The phone rings.

The set re-illumines to reveal CYNTHIA, FELICITY *and* MAGNUS *about to take coffee, which is being taken round by* MRS. DRUDGE. SIMON *is missing. The body lies in position.*

MRS. DRUDGE (*into phone*): The same, half an hour later? . . . No, I'm sorry—there's no one of that name here. (*She replaces phone and goes round with coffee. To* CYNTHIA.) Black or white, my lady?

CYNTHIA: White please.

MRS. DRUDGE *pours.*

MRS. DRUDGE (*to* FELICITY): Black or white, miss?

FELICITY: White please.

MRS. DRUDGE *pours.*

MRS. DRUDGE (*to* MAGNUS): Black or white, Major?

MAGNUS: White please.

Ditto.

MRS. DRUDGE (*to* CYNTHIA): Sugar, my lady?

CYNTHIA: Yes please.

Puts sugar in.

MRS. DRUDGE (*to* FELICITY): Sugar, miss?

FELICITY: Yes please.

Ditto.

MRS. DRUDGE (*to* MAGNUS): Sugar, Major?

MAGNUS: Yes please.

Ditto.

MRS. DRUDGE *leaves, and reappears with a plate of biscuits.*

MRS. DRUDGE (*to* CYNTHIA): Biscuit, my lady?

CYNTHIA: No thank you.

BIRDBOOT (*writing elaborately in his notebook*): The second act, however, fails to fulfill the promise . . .

FELICITY: If you ask me, there's something funny going on.

Mrs. Drudge's approach to FELICITY makes FELICITY jump to her feet in impatience. She goes to the radio while MAGNUS declines his biscuit, and MRS. DRUDGE leaves.

RADIO: We interrupt our programme for a special police message. The search for the dangerous madman who is on the loose in Essex has now narrowed to the immediate vicinity of Muldoon Manor. Police are hampered by the deadly swamps and the fog, but believe that the madman spent last night in a deserted cottage on the cliffs. The public is advised to stick together and make sure none of their number is missing. That is the end of the police message.

FELICITY *turns off the radio nervously. Pause.*

CYNTHIA: Where's Simon?

FELICITY: Who?

CYNTHIA: Simon. Have you seen him?

FELICITY: No.

CYNTHIA: Have you, Magnus?

MAGNUS: No.

CYNTHIA: Oh.

FELICITY: Yes, there's something foreboding in the air, it is as if one of *us*—

CYNTHIA: Oh, Felicity, the house is locked up tight—no one can get in—and the police are practically on the doorstep.

FELICITY: I don't know—it's just a feeling.

CYNTHIA: It's only the fog.

MAGNUS: Hound will never get through on a day like this—

CYNTHIA (*shouting at him*): *Fog!*

FELICITY: He means the Inspector.

CYNTHIA: Is he bringing a dog?

FELICITY: Not that I know of.

MAGNUS: —never get through the swamps. Yes, I'm afraid the madman can show his hand in safety now.

A mournful baying, hooting is heard in the distance, scary.

CYNTHIA: What's that?!

FELICITY (*tensely*): It sounded like the cry of a gigantic hound!

BIRDBOOT: Rings a bell.

MAGNUS: Poor devil!

CYNTHIA: Ssssh!

They listen. The sound is repeated, nearer.

FELICITY: There it is again!

CYNTHIA: It's coming this way—it's right outside the house!

MRS. DRUDGE *enters.*

MRS. DRUDGE: Inspector Hound!

CYNTHIA: A *police* dog?

Enter INSPECTOR HOUND. *On his feet are his swamp boots. These are two inflatable—and inflated—pontoons with flat bottoms about two feet across. He carries a foghorn.*

HOUND: Lady Muldoon?

CYNTHIA: Yes.

HOUND: I came as soon as I could. Where shall I put my foghorn and my swamp boots?

CYNTHIA: Mrs. Drudge will take them out. Be prepared, as the Force's motto has it, eh, Inspector? How very resourceful!

HOUND (*divesting himself of boots and foghorn*): It takes more than a bit of weather to keep a policeman from his duty.

MRS. DRUDGE *leaves with chattels. A pause.*

CYNTHIA: Oh—er, Inspector Hound—Felicity Cunningham, Major Magnus Muldoon.

HOUND: Good evening.

He and CYNTHIA *continue to look expectantly at each other.*

CYNTHIA *and* HOUND (*together*): Well?—Sorry—

CYNTHIA: No, do go on.

HOUND: Thank you. Well, tell me about it in your own words—take your time, begin at the beginning and don't leave anything out.

CYNTHIA: I beg your pardon?

HOUND: Fear nothing. You are in safe hands now. I hope you haven't touched anything.

CYNTHIA: I'm afraid I don't understand.

HOUND: I'm Inspector Hound.

CYNTHIA: Yes.

HOUND: Well, what's it all about?

CYNTHIA: I really have no idea.

HOUND: How did it begin?

CYNTHIA: What?

HOUND: The . . . thing.

CYNTHIA: What thing?

HOUND (*rapidly losing confidence but exasperated*): The trouble!

CYNTHIA: There hasn't *been* any trouble!

HOUND: Didn't you phone the police?

CYNTHIA: No.

FELICITY: I didn't.

MAGNUS: What for?

HOUND: I see. (*Pause.*) This puts me in a very difficult position. (*A steady pause.*) Well, I'll be getting along, then. (*He moves towards the door.*)

CYNTHIA: I'm terribly sorry.

HOUND (*stiffly*): That's perfectly all right.

CYNTHIA: Thank you so much for coming.

HOUND: Not at all. You never know, there might have been a serious matter.

CYNTHIA: Drink?

HOUND: More serious than that, even.

CYNTHIA (*correcting*): Drink before you go?

HOUND: No thank you. (*Leaves.*)

CYNTHIA (*through the door*): I do hope you find him.

HOUND (*reappearing at once*): Find who, Madam?— out with it!

CYNTHIA: I thought you were looking for the lunatic.

HOUND: And what do you know about that?

CYNTHIA: It was on the radio.

HOUND: Was it, indeed? Well, that's what I'm here about, really. I didn't want to mention it because I didn't know how much you knew. No point in causing unnecessary panic, even with a murderer in our midst.

FELICITY: Murderer, did you say?

HOUND: Ah—so that was not on the radio?

CYNTHIA: Whom has he murdered, Inspector?

HOUND: Perhaps no one—yet. Let us hope we are in time.

MAGNUS: You believe he is in our midst, Inspector?

HOUND: I do. If anyone of you have recently encountered a youngish good-looking fellow in a smart suit, white shirt, hatless, well-spoken—someone possibly claiming to have just moved into the neighbourhood, someone who on the surface seems as sane as you or I, then now is the time to speak!

FELICITY: . . . I . . .

HOUND: Don't interrupt!

FELICITY: Inspector . . .

HOUND: Very well.

CYNTHIA: No. Felicity!

HOUND: Please, Lady Cynthia, we are all in this together. I must ask you to put yourself completely in my hands.

CYNTHIA: Don't, Inspector. I love Albert.

HOUND: I don't think you quite grasp my meaning.

MAGNUS: Is one of us in danger, Inspector?

HOUND: Didn't it strike you as odd that on his escape the madman made a beeline for Muldoon Manor? It is my guess that he bears a deep-seated grudge against someone in this very house! Lady Muldoon—where is your husband?

CYNTHIA: My husband?—you don't mean—?

HOUND: I don't know—but I have a reason to believe that one of you is the real McCoy!

FELICITY: The real what?

HOUND: William Herbert McCoy who as a young man, meeting the madman in the street and being solicited for sixpence for a cup of tea, replied,

"Why don't you do a decent day's work, you shifty old bag of horse manure," in Canada all those many years ago and went on to make his fortune. (*He starts to pace intensely.*) The madman was a mere boy at the time but he never forgot that moment, and thenceforth carried in his heart the promise of revenge! (*At which point he finds himself standing on top of the corpse. He looks down carefully.*) Is there anything you have forgotten to tell me?

They all see the corpse for the first time.

FELICITY: So the madman has struck!

CYNTHIA: Oh—it's horrible—horrible—

HOUND: Yes, just as I feared. Now you see the sort of man you are protecting.

CYNTHIA: I can't believe it!

FELICITY: I'll have to tell him, Cynthia—Inspector, a stranger of that description has indeed appeared in our midst—Simon Gascoyne. Oh, he had charm, I'll give you that, and he took me in completely. I'm afraid I made a fool of myself over him, and so did Cynthia.

HOUND: Where is he now?

MAGNUS: He must be around the house—he couldn't get away in these conditions.

HOUND: You're right. Fear naught, Lady Muldoon—I shall apprehend the man who killed your husband.

CYNTHIA: My husband? I don't understand.

HOUND: Everything points to Gascoyne.

CYNTHIA: But who's that? (*The corpse.*)

HOUND: Your husband.

CYNTHIA: No, it's not.

HOUND: Yes, it is.

CYNTHIA: I tell you it's not.

HOUND: Are you sure?

CYNTHIA: For goodness sake!

HOUND: Then who is it?

CYNTHIA: I don't know.

HOUND: Anybody?

FELICITY: I've never seen him before.

MAGNUS: Quite unlike anybody I've ever met.

HOUND: I seem to have made a dreadful mistake. Lady Muldoon, I do apologize.

CYNTHIA: But what are we going to do?

HOUND (*snatching the phone*): I'll phone the police!

CYNTHIA: But you are the police!

HOUND: Thank God I'm here—the lines have been cut!

CYNTHIA: You mean—?

HOUND: Yes!—we're on our own, cut off from the world and in grave danger!

FELICITY: You mean—?

HOUND: Yes!—I think the killer will strike again!

MAGNUS: You mean—?

HOUND: Yes! One of us ordinary mortals thrown together by fate and cut off by the elements, is the murderer! He must be found—search the house!

All depart speedily in different directions leaving a momentarily empty stage. SIMON *strolls on.*

SIMON (*entering, calling*): Anyone about?—funny . . . (*He notices the corpse and is surprised. He approaches it and turns it over. He stands up and looks about in alarm.*)

BIRDBOOT: This is where Simon gets the chap.

There is a shot. SIMON *falls dead.*

INSPECTOR HOUND *runs on and crouches down by Simon's body.* CYNTHIA *appears at the French windows. She stops there and stares.*

CYNTHIA: What happened, Inspector?!

HOUND *turns to face her.*

HOUND: He's dead . . . Simon Gascoyne, I presume. Rough justice even for a killer—unless—unless—We assumed that the body could not have been lying there before Simon Gascoyne entered the house . . . but . . . (*he slides the sofa over the body*) . . . there's your answer. And now—who killed Simon Gascoyne? And why?

"Curtain," Freeze, Applause, Exeunt.

MOON: Why not?

BIRDBOOT: Exactly. Good riddance.

MOON: Yes, getting away with murder must be quite easy provided that one's motive is sufficiently inscrutable.

BIRDBOOT: Fickle young pup! He was deceiving her right, left and centre.

MOON (*thoughtfully*): Of course, I'd still have Puckeridge behind *me* . . .

BIRDBOOT: She needs someone steadier, more mature . . .

MOON: . . . And if I could, so could he . . .

BIRDBOOT: Yes, I know of this rather nice hotel, very discreet, run by a man of the world. . . .

MOON: Uneasy lies the head that wears the crown.

BIRDBOOT: Breakfast served in one's room and no questions asked.

MOON: Does Puckeridge dream of me?

BIRDBOOT (*pause*): Hello—what's happened?

MOON: What? Oh yes—what do you make of it, so far?

BIRDBOOT (*clears throat*): It is at this point that the play, for me, comes alive. The groundwork has been well and truly laid, and the author has taken the trouble to learn from the masters of the genre. He has created a real situation, and few will doubt his ability to resolve it with a startling dénouement. Certainly that is what it so far lacks, but it has a beginning, a middle and I have no doubt it will prove to have an end. For this let us give thanks, and double thanks for a good clean show without a trace of smut. But perhaps even all this would be for nothing were it not for a performance which I consider to be one of the summits in the range of contemporary theatre. In what is possibly the finest Cynthia since the war—

MOON: If we examine this more closely, and I think close examination is the least tribute that this play deserves, I think we will find that within the austere framework of what is seen to be on one level a country-house week-end, and what a useful symbol that is, the author has given us—yes, I will go so far—he has given us the human condition—

BIRDBOOT: More talent in her little finger—

MOON: An uncanny ear that might have belonged to a Van Gogh—

BIRDBOOT: —a public scandal that the Birthday Honours to date have neglected—

MOON: Faced as we are with such ubiquitous obliquity, it is hard, it is hard indeed, and therefore I will not attempt, to refrain from invoking the names of Kafka, Sartre, Shakespeare, St. Paul, Beckett, Birkett, Pinero, Pirandello, Dante and Dorothy L. Sayers.

BIRDBOOT: A rattling good evening out. I was held.

The phone starts to ring on the empty stage. MOON *tries to ignore it.*

MOON: Harder still— Harder still if possible— Harder still if it is possible to be— Neither do I find it easy— Dante and Dorothy L. Sayers. Harder still—

BIRDBOOT: Others taking part included—*Moon!*

For MOON *has lost patience and is bearing down on the ringing phone. He is frankly irritated.*

MOON (*picking up phone, barks*): Hel-lo! (*Pause, turns to* BIRDBOOT, *quietly.*) It's for you.

Pause.

BIRDBOOT *gets up. He approaches cautiously.* MOON *gives him the phone and moves back to his seat.* BIRDBOOT *watches him go. He looks round and smiles weakly, expiating himself.*

BIRDBOOT (*into phone*): Hello. . . . (*Explosion.*) Oh, for God's sake, Myrtle—I've told you never to phone me at work! (*He is naturally embarrassed, looking about with surreptitious fury.*) What? Last night? Good God, woman, this is hardly the time to—I assure you, Myrtle, there is absolutely nothing going on between me and—. I took her to dinner simply by way of keeping *au fait* with the world of the paint and the motley—yes, I promise—Yes, I do—Yes, I *said* yes—I *do*—and you are mine too, Myrtle—darling—I can't—(*whispers*) *I'm not alone* —(*Up.*) No, she's not!—(*He looks around furtively, licks his lips and mumbles.*) All *right!* I love your

43

little pink ears and you are my own fluffy bunny-boo— Now for God's sake— Good-bye, Myrtle—(*puts down phone*).

BIRDBOOT *mops his brow with his handkerchief. As he turns, a tennis ball bounces in through the French windows, followed by* FELICITY, *as before, in tennis outfit. The lighting is as it was. Everything is as it was. It is, let us say, the same moment of time.*

FELICITY (*calling*): Out! (*She catches sight of* BIRDBOOT *and is amazed.*) You!

BIRDBOOT: Er, yes—hello again.

FELICITY: What are you doing here?!

BIRDBOOT: Well, I . . .

FELICITY: Honestly, darling, you really are extraordi-nary—

BIRDBOOT: Yes, well, here I am. (*He looks round sheep-ishly.*)

FELICITY: You must have been desperate to see me—I mean, I'm flattered, but couldn't it wait till I got back?

BIRDBOOT: No, no, you've got it all wrong—

FELICITY: What is it?

BIRDBOOT: And about last night—perhaps I gave you the wrong impression—got carried away a bit, per-haps—

FELICITY (*stiffly*): What are you trying to say?

BIRDBOOT: I want to call it off.

FELICITY: I see.

BIRDBOOT: I didn't promise anything—and the fact is, I have my reputation—people do talk—

FELICITY: You don't have to say any more—

BIRDBOOT: And my wife, too—I don't know how she got to hear of it, but—

FELICITY: Of all the nerve!

BIRDBOOT: I'm sorry you had to find out like this—the fact is I didn't mean it this way—

FELICITY: You philandering coward!

BIRDBOOT: I'm sorry—but I want you to know that I meant those things I said—oh yes—shows brilliant promise—I shall say so—

FELICITY: I'll kill you for this, Simon Gascoyne!

She leaves in tears, passing MRS. DRUDGE *who has entered in time to overhear her last remark.*

BIRDBOOT (*wide-eyed*): Good God . . .

MRS. DRUDGE: I have come to set up the card table, sir.

BIRDBOOT (*wildly*): I can't stay for a game of *cards!*

MRS. DRUDGE: Oh, Lady Muldoon *will* be disappointed.

BIRDBOOT: You mean . . . you mean, she wants to meet me . . . ?

MRS. DRUDGE: Oh yes, sir, I just told her and it put her in quite a tizzy.

BIRDBOOT: Really? Yes, well, a man of my influence is not to be sneezed at—I think I have some small name for the making of reputations—mmm, yes, quite a tizzy, you say?

MRS. DRUDGE *is busied with the card table.* BIRDBOOT *stands marooned and bemused for a moment.*

MOON (*from his seat*): Birdboot!—(*a tense whisper*)— Birdboot!

BIRDBOOT *looks round vaguely.*

What the hell are you doing?

BIRDBOOT: Nothing.

MOON: Stop making an ass of yourself. Come back.

BIRDBOOT: Oh, I know what you're thinking—but the fact is I genuinely consider her performance to be one of the summits—

CYNTHIA *enters as before.* MRS. DRUDGE *has gone.*

CYNTHIA: Darling!

BIRDBOOT: Ah, good evening—may I say that I genuinely consider—

CYNTHIA: Don't say anything for a moment—just hold me. (*She falls into his arms.*)

BIRDBOOT: All right!—let us throw off the hollow pretences of the gimcrack codes we live by! Dear lady, from the first moment I saw you, I felt my whole life changing—

CYNTHIA (*breaking free*): We can't go on meeting like this!

BIRDBOOT: I am not ashamed to proclaim nightly my love for you!—but fortunately that will not be necessary—I know of a very good hotel, discreet—run by a man of the world—

CYNTHIA: But darling, this is madness!

BIRDBOOT: Yes! I am mad with love.

CYNTHIA: Please!—remember where we are!

BIRDBOOT: I don't care! Let them think what they like, I love you!

CYNTHIA: Don't—I love Albert!

BIRDBOOT: He's dead. (*Shaking her.*) Do you understand me—Albert's dead!

CYNTHIA: No—I'll never give up hope! Let me go! We are not free!

BIRDBOOT: You mean Myrtle? She means nothing to me—

nothing!—she's all cocoa and blue nylon fur slip-
pers—not a spark of creative genius in her whole
slumping knee-length-knickered body—
CYNTHIA: You're a cad, Simon! You will use me and cast
me aside as you have cast aside so many others!
BIRDBOOT: No, Cynthia—now that I have found you—
CYNTHIA: You're ruthless—so strong—so cruel—

> BIRDBOOT *seizes her in an embrace, during which*
> MRS. DRUDGE *enters, and Moon's fevered voice is*
> *heard.*

MOON: Have you taken leave of your tiny mind?

> CYNTHIA *breaks free.*

CYNTHIA: Stop—can't you see you're making a fool of
yourself!
MOON: She's right.
BIRDBOOT (*to* MOON): You keep out of this.
CYNTHIA: Yes, what is it, Mrs. Drudge?
MRS. DRUDGE: Should I close the windows, my lady? The
fog—
CYNTHIA: Yes, you'd better.
MOON: Look, they've got your number—
BIRDBOOT: I'll leave in my own time, thank you very
much.
MOON: It's the finish of you, I suppose you know that—
BIRDBOOT: I don't need your twopenny Grubb Street
prognostications—I have found something bigger
and finer—
MOON (*bemused, to himself*): If only it were Higgs. . .
CYNTHIA: . . . And fetch the Major down.
MRS. DRUDGE: I think I hear him coming downstairs
now.

She leaves. The sound of a wheelchair's approach as before. BIRDBOOT *prudently keeps out of the chair's former path but it enters from the next wing down and knocks him flying. A babble of anguish and protestation.*

CYNTHIA: Simon—say something!
BIRDBOOT: That reckless bastard (*as he sits up*).
CYNTHIA: Thank God!—
MAGNUS: What's *he* doing here?
CYNTHIA: He just turned up.
MAGNUS: Really? How do you like it here?
BIRDBOOT: I couldn't take it night after night.
> FELICITY *enters.*
FELICITY: So—you're still here.
CYNTHIA: Of course he's still here. We're going to play cards. There is no need to introduce you two, is there, for I recall now that you, Simon, met me through Felicity, our mutual friend.
FELICITY: Yes, Simon is an old friend . . .
BIRDBOOT: Ah—yes—well I like to give young up-and-comers the benefit of my—er—of course, she lacks technique as yet—
FELICITY: Last night.
BIRDBOOT: I'm not talking about last night!
CYNTHIA: Indeed? Well, you deal, Felicity. Simon, you help me with the sofa.

CYNTHIA *and* MAGNUS *confer as in the earlier scene.*

BIRDBOOT (*to* MOON): Did you see that? Tried to kill me. I told you it was Magnus—not that it *is* Magnus.
MOON: Who did it, you mean?
BIRDBOOT: What?
MOON: You think it's not Magnus who did it?

BIRDBOOT: Get a grip on yourself, Moon—the facts are staring you in the face. He's after Cynthia for one thing.

MAGNUS: It's Gascoyne, isn't it?

BIRDBOOT: Over my dead body!

MAGNUS: If he comes between us . . .

MOON (*angrily*): For God's sake sit down!

CYNTHIA: Simon!

BIRDBOOT: She needs me, Moon. I've got to make up a four.

CYNTHIA *and* BIRDBOOT *move the sofa as before, and they all sit at the table.*

CYNTHIA: Right! Who starts?

MAGNUS: I do. I'll dummy for a no-bid ruff and double my holding on South's queen (*while he moves cards*).

CYNTHIA: Did I hear you say you saw Felicity last night, Simon?

BIRDBOOT: Er—er—

FELICITY: Pay twenty-ones or trump my contract. (*Discards.*) Cynthia's turn.

CYNTHIA: I'll trump your contract with five dummy no-trumps there (*discards*), and I'll move West's rook for the re-bid with a banker ruff on his second trick there. (*Discards.*) Simon?

BIRDBOOT: Would you mind doing that again?

CYNTHIA: And I'll ruff your dummy with five no-bid trumps there (*discards*), and I support your re-bid with a banker for the solo ruff in the dummy trick there. (*Discards.*)

BIRDBOOT (*standing up and throwing down his cards*): And I call your bluff!

CYNTHIA: Well done, Simon!

MAGNUS *pays* BIRDBOOT *while* CYNTHIA *deals.*

FELICITY: Strange how Simon appeared in the neighbourhood from nowhere, we know so little about him.

CYNTHIA: Right Simon, it's your opening on the minor bid. Hmm. Let's see. I think I'll overbid the spade convention with two no trumps and King's gambit offered there—(*discards*) and West's dummy split double to Queen's Bishop 4 there!

MAGNUS (*as he plays cards*): Faites vos jeux. Rien ne va plus. Rouge et noir. Zéro.

CYNTHIA: Simon?

BIRDBOOT (*triumphant, leaping to his feet*): And I call your bluff!

CYNTHIA (*imperturbably*): I meld.

FELICITY: I huff.

MAGNUS: I ruff.

BIRDBOOT: I bluff.

CYNTHIA: Twist.

FELICITY: Bust.

MAGNUS: Check.

BIRDBOOT: Snap.

CYNTHIA: How's that?

FELICITY: Not out.

MAGNUS: Double top.

BIRDBOOT: Bingo!

Climax.

CYNTHIA: No! Simon—your luck's in tonight.

FELICITY: We shall see—the night is not over yet, Simon Gascoyne! (*She exits quickly.*)

BIRDBOOT (*looking after* FELICITY): Red herring—smell

it a mile off. (*To* MAGNUS.) Oh yes, she's as clean as a whistle, I've seen it a thousand times. And I've seen you before too, haven't I? Strange—there's something about you . . .

MAGNUS: Care for a spin round the rose garden, Cynthia?

CYNTHIA: No Magnus, I must talk to Simon.

BIRDBOOT: There's nothing for you there, you know.

MAGNUS: You think so?

BIRDBOOT: Oh yes, she knows which side her bread is buttered. I am a man not without a certain influence among those who would reap the limelight—she's not going to throw me over for a heavily disguised cripple.

MAGNUS: There's an old Canadian proverb—

BIRDBOOT: Don't give me that—I tumbled to you right from the start—oh yes, you chaps are not as clever as you think. . . . Sooner or later you make your mistake. . . . Incidentally, where was it I saw you? . . . I've definitely. . . .

CYNTHIA (*calling*): Simon!

MAGNUS (*leaving*): Well, I think I'll go and oil my gun. (*Exit.*)

BIRDBOOT (*after* MAGNUS): Double bluff!—(*To* CYNTHIA.) I've seen it a thousand times.

CYNTHIA: I think Magnus suspects something. And Felicity . . . Simon, was there anything between you and Felicity?

BIRDBOOT: No, no—that's all over now. I merely flattered her a little over a drink, told her she'd go far, that sort of thing. Dear me, the fuss that's been made over a simple flirtation—

CYNTHIA (*as* MRS. DRUDGE *enters behind*): If I find you

have falsely seduced me from my dear husband Albert, I will kill you, Simon Gascoyne!

The "Curtain" as before. MRS. DRUDGE *and* CYNTHIA *leave.* BIRDBOOT *starts to follow them.*

MOON: *Birdboot!*

BIRDBOOT *stops.*

MOON: For God's sake pull yourself together.

BIRDBOOT: I can't help it.

MOON: What do you think you're doing? You're turning it into a complete farce!

BIRDBOOT: I know, I know—but I can't live without her. (*He is making erratic neurotic journeys about the stage.*) I shall resign my position, of course. I don't care I'm a goner, I tell you—(*He has arrived at the body. He looks at it in surprise, hesitates, bends and turns it over.*)

MOON: Birdboot, think of your family, your friends—your high standing in the world of letters—I say, what are you doing?

BIRDBOOT *is staring at the body's face.*

Birdboot . . . leave it alone. Come and sit down—what's the matter with you?

BIRDBOOT (*dead-voiced*): It's Higgs.

MOON: What?

BIRDBOOT: It's Higgs.

Pause.

MOON: Don't be silly.

BIRDBOOT: I tell you it's Higgs!

MOON *half-rises. Bewildered.*

I don't understand . . . He's dead.

MOON: Dead?

BIRDBOOT: Who would want to . . .

MOON: He must have been lying there all the time. . . .

BIRDBOOT: . . . kill Higgs?

MOON: But what's he doing here? I was standing in tonight. . . .

BIRDBOOT (*turning*): Moon? . . .

MOON (*in wonder, quietly*): So it's me and Puckeridge now.

BIRDBOOT: Moon . . . ?

MOON (*faltering*): But I swear I . . .

BIRDBOOT: I've got it—

MOON: But I didn't—

BIRDBOOT (*quietly*): My God . . . so that was it. . . . (*Up.*) Moon—now I see—

MOON: —I swear I didn't—

BIRDBOOT: Now—finally—I see it all—

There is a shot and BIRDBOOT *falls dead.*

MOON: Birdboot! (*He runs on, to Birdboot's body.*)

CYNTHIA *appears at the French windows. She stops and stares. All as before.*

CYNTHIA: Oh my God—what happened, Inspector?

MOON (*almost to himself*): He's dead. . . . (*He rises.*) That's a bit rough, isn't it?—a bit extreme!—He may have had his faults—I admit he was a fickle old . . . Who did this, and why?

MOON *turns to face her. He stands up and makes swiftly for his seat. Before he gets there he is stopped by the sound of voices.* SIMON *and* HOUND *are occupying the critics' seats.* MOON *freezes.*

SIMON: To say that it is without pace, point, focus, interest, drama, wit or originality is to say simply that it does not happen to be my cup of tea. One has only to compare this ragbag with the masters of the genre to see that here we have a trifle that is not my cup of tea at all.

HOUND: I'm sorry to be blunt but there is no getting away from it. It lacks pace. A complete ragbag.

SIMON: I will go further. Those of you who were fortunate enough to be at the Comédie-Française on Wednesday last, will not need to be reminded that hysterics are no substitute for *éclat*.

HOUND: It lacks *élan*.

SIMON: Some of the cast seem to have given up acting altogether, apparently aghast, with every reason, at finding themselves involved in an evening that would, and indeed will, make the angels weep.

HOUND: I am not a prude but I fail to see any reason for the shower of filth and sexual allusion foisted onto an unsuspected public in the guise of modernity at all costs. . . .

Behind MOON, FELICITY, MAGNUS *and* MRS. DRUDGE *have made their entrances, so that he turns to face their semicircle.*

MAGNUS (*pointing to Birdboot's body*): Well, Inspector, is this your man?

MOON (*warily*): . . . Yes. . . . Yes. . . .

CYNTHIA: It's Simon . . .

MOON: Yes . . . yes . . . poor. . . . (*Up*) Is this some kind of a joke?

MAGNUS: If it is, Inspector, it's in very poor taste.

MOON *pulls himself together and becomes galvanic, a little wild, in grief for* BIRDBOOT.

MOON: All right! I'm going to find out who did this! I want everyone to go to the positions they occupied when the shot was fired—

They move; hysterically.

No one will leave the house!

They move back.

MAGNUS: I think we all had the opportunity to fire the shot, Inspector—

MOON (*furious*): I am not—

MAGNUS: —but which of us would want to?

MOON: Perhaps you, Major Magnus!

MAGNUS: Why should I want to kill him?

MOON: Because he was on to you—yes, he tumbled you right from the start—and you shot him just when he was about to reveal that you killed—(MOON *points, pauses and then crosses to Higgs' body and falters*)—killed—(*he turns* HIGGS *over*) . . . this . . . chap.

MAGNUS: But what motive would there be for killing him? (*Pause.*) Who *is* this chap? (*Pause.*) Inspector?

MOON (*rising*): I don't know. Quite unlike anyone I've ever met. (*Long pause.*) Well . . . now . . .

MRS. DRUDGE: Inspector?

MOON (*eagerly*): Yes? Yes, what is it, dear lady?

MRS. DRUDGE: Happening to enter this room earlier in the day to close the windows, I chanced to overhear a remark made by the deceased Simon Gascoyne to her ladyship, viz., "I will kill anyone who comes between us."

MOON: Ah—yes—well, that's it, then. This . . . chap . . . (*pointing to the body*) was obviously killed by (*pointing to Birdboot's body*) er . . . (*the moment of Moon's betrayal, for which he is to pay with his life*) . . . by (*pause*) Simon.

CYNTHIA: But he didn't come between us!

MAGNUS: And who, then, killed Simon?

MRS. DRUDGE: Subsequent to that reported remark, I also happened to be in earshot of a remark made by Lady Muldoon to the deceased, to the effect, "I will kill you, Simon Gascoyne!" I hope you don't mind my mentioning it.

MOON: Not at all. I'm glad you did. It is from these chance remarks that we in the Force build up our complete picture before moving in to make the arrest. It will not be long now, I fancy, and I must warn you, Lady Muldoon that anything you say—

CYNTHIA: Yes!—I hated Simon Gascoyne, for he had me in his thrall!—But I didn't kill him!

MRS. DRUDGE: Prior to that, Inspector, I also chanced to overhear a remark made by Miss Cunningham, no doubt in the heat of the moment, but it stuck in my mind as these things do, viz., "I will kill you for this, Simon Gascoyne!"

MOON: Ah! The final piece of the jigsaw! I think I am now in a position to reveal the mystery. This man (*the corpse*) was, of course, McCoy, the Canadian who, as we heard, meeting Gascoyne in the street and being solicited for sixpence for a toffee apple, smacked him across the ear, with the cry, "How's that for a grudge to harbour, you sniffling little workshy!" all those many years ago. Gascoyne bided his time, but in due course tracked McCoy down to this house, having, on the way, met, in the neighbourhood, a simple ambitious girl from the provinces. He was charming, persuasive—told her, I have no doubt, that she would go straight to the top—and she, flattered by his sophistication, taken in by his promises to see her all right on the night, gave in to his simple desires. Perhaps she loved him. We shall never know. But in the very hour of her promised triumph, his eye fell on another—yes, I refer to Lady Cynthia Muldoon. From the moment he caught sight of her there was no other woman for him—he was in her spell, willing to sacrifice anything, even you, Felicity Cunningham. It was only today—unexpectedly finding him here—that you learned the truth. There was a bitter argument which ended with your promise to kill him—a promise that you carried out in this very room at your first opportunity! And I must warn you that anything you say—

FELICITY: But it doesn't make sense!

MOON: Not at first glance, *perhaps*.

MAGNUS: Could not McCoy have been killed by the same person who killed Simon?

FELICITY: But why should any of us want to kill a perfect stranger?

MAGNUS: Perhaps he was not a stranger to *one* of us.

MOON (*faltering*): But Simon was the madman, wasn't he?

MAGNUS: We only have your word for that, Inspector. We only have your word for a lot of things. For instance—McCoy. Who is he? Is his name McCoy? Is there any truth in that fantastic and implausible tale of the insult inflicted in the Canadian streets? Or is there something else, something quite unknown to us, behind all this? Suppose for a moment that the madman, having killed this unknown stranger for private and inscrutable reasons of his own, was disturbed before he could dispose of the body, so having cut the telephone wires he decided to return to the scene of the crime, masquerading as—Police Inspector Hound!

MOON: But . . . I'm not mad . . . I'm almost sure I'm not mad . . .

MAGNUS: . . . only to discover that in the house was a man, Simon Gascoyne, who recognized the corpse as a man against whom you had held a deep-seated grudge—!

MOON: But I didn't kill—I'm almost sure I—

MAGNUS: I put it to you!—are you the real Inspector Hound?!

MOON: You know damn well I'm not! What's it all about?

MAGNUS: I thought as much.

MOON: I only dreamed . . . sometimes I dreamed—

CYNTHIA: So it was you!

MRS. DRUDGE: The madman!

FELICITY: The killer!

CYNTHIA: Oh, it's horrible, horrible.

MRS. DRUDGE: The stranger in our midst!

MAGNUS: Yes, we had a shrewd suspicion he would turn up here—and he walked into the trap!

MOON: What *trap?*

MAGNUS: I am not the real Magnus Muldoon—It was a mere subterfuge!—and (*standing up and removing his moustaches*) I now reveal myself as—

CYNTHIA: You mean—?

MAGNUS: Yes! I am the real Inspector Hound!

MOON (*pause*): *Puckeridge!*

MAGNUS (*with pistol*): Stand where you are, or I shoot!

MOON (*backing*): Puckeridge! You killed Higgs—and Birdboot tried to tell me—

MAGNUS: Stop in the name of the law!

> MOON *turns to run.* MAGNUS *fires.* MOON *drops to his knees.*

I have waited a long time for this moment.

CYNTHIA: So you are the real Inspector Hound.

MAGNUS: Not only that!—I have been leading a double life—at *least!*

CYNTHIA: You mean—?

MAGNUS: Yes!—It's been ten long years, but don't you know me?

CYNTHIA: You mean—?

MAGNUS: Yes!—it is me, Albert!—who lost his memory and joined the Force, rising by merit to the rank of Inspector, his past blotted out—until fate cast him back into the home he left behind, back to the beautiful woman he had brought here as his girlish bride—in short, my darling, my memory has returned and your long wait is over!

CYNTHIA: Oh, Albert!

> *They embrace.*

MOON (*with a trace of admiration*): Puckeridge! . . . you cunning bastard. (*He dies.*)

THE END

AFTER MAGRITTE

The first performance of AFTER MAGRITTE was given at the Ambiance Lunch-hour Theatre Club on 9th April 1970. The cast was as follows:

FOOT	Clive Barker
HOLMES	Malcolm Ingram
HARRIS	Stephen Moore
THELMA	Prunella Scales
MOTHER	Josephine Tewson

Directed by Geoffrey Reeves

Characters

HARRIS   aged about 40
THELMA   his wife, a bit younger, attractive
MOTHER   a little old, tough, querulous lady
FOOT   Detective Inspector
HOLMES   Police Constable

SCENE

A room. Early evening.

The only light is that which comes through the large window which is facing the audience. The street door is in the same upstage wall. There is another door on each side of the stage, leading to the rest of the flat.

The central ceiling light hangs from a long flex which disappears up into the flies. The lampshade itself is a heavy metal hemisphere, opaque, poised about eight feet from the floor.

A yard or more to one side (Stage L*), and similarly hanging from the flies, is a fruit basket attractively overflowing with apples, oranges, bananas, pineapple, and grapes. The cord or flex is tied round the handle of the basket.*

It will become apparent that the light fixture is on a counterweight system; it can be raised or lowered, or kept in any vertical position, by means of the counterbalance, which in this case is a basket of fruit.

Most of the furniture is stacked up against the street door in a sort of barricade. An essential item is a long low bench-type table, about eight feet long, but the pile also includes a settee, two comfortable chairs, a TV set, a cupboard and a wind-up gramophone with an old-fashioned horn. The cupboard is probably the item on which stand the telephone and a deep-shaded table lamp, unlit but connected to a wall plug.

Directly under the central light is a wooden chair. Hanging over the back of the chair is a black tail-coat, a white dress shirt and a white bow-tie. Towards Stage R, *in profile, is an ironing board with its iron upended on the asbestos mat at the centre-stage end of the board.*

There is no other furniture.

There are three people in the room.

MOTHER *is lying on her back on the ironing board, her head to Stage* R, *her downstage foot up against the flat of the iron. A white bath towel covers her from ankle to chin. Her head and part of her face are concealed in a tight-fitting black rubber bathing cap. A black bowler hat reposes on her stomach. She could be dead; but is not.*

THELMA HARRIS *is dressed in a full-length ballgown and her hair is expensively "up". She looks as though she is ready to go out to a dance, which she is. Her silver shoes, however, are not on her feet: they have been discarded somewhere on the floor.* THELMA *is discovered on her hands and knees, in profile to the audience, staring at the floor ahead and giving vent to an occasional sniff.*

REGINALD HARRIS *is standing on the wooden chair. His torso is bare, but underneath his thigh-length green rubber fishing waders he wears his black evening dress trousers. His hands are at his sides. His head is tilted back directly below the lampshade, which hangs a foot or two above him and he is blowing slowly and deliberately up into the recess of the shade.*

Gazing at this scene through the window is a uniformed

Police Constable (HOLMES). *Only his shoulders, his face and his helmet are visible above the sill. He stands absolutely motionless, and might be a cut-out figure; but is not.*

For several seconds there is no movement, and no sound save the occasional blowing from HARRIS *and the occasional sniffing from* THELMA. THELMA *pads forward a couple of paces, still scanning the floor ahead and around.* HARRIS *blows into the lampshade.*

Without looking up at HARRIS, THELMA *speaks.*

THELMA: It's electric, dear.
HARRIS: (*mildly*) I didn't think it was a flaming torch.
THELMA: There's no need to use language. That's what I
      always say.
      (*She pads on a bit, scanning the floor.* HARRIS
      *tries to remove the light bulb but it is apparently
      still too hot: he blows on his sharply withdrawn
      fingers, and then continues to blow on the light
      bulb. After a couple of blows he tests the bulb
      again and is able to remove it.*)
      (*This upsets the delicate balance of the counter-
      weight. The shade, relieved of the weight of the
      bulb, slowly begins to ascend, while the basket of
      fruit descends accordingly.* HARRIS, *however, has
      anticipated this and the movement is one of only
      a few inches before he has turned on his chair
      and removed an apple from the basket. This
      reverses the effect: the basket ascends, the shade
      descends. But* HARRIS *has anticipated this also:*

*he takes a bite out of the apple and replaces it.
The equilibrium is thus restored.*)
You could have used your handkerchief.

HARRIS: (*intrigued*) You mean, *semaphor*?

(*But* THELMA *is not listening: she has given up her
search, stood up, approached her shoes—and
stepped on something; it is in fact a lead slug
from a .22 calibre pistol. She picks it up with
satisfaction and tosses it into a metal wastebin
wherein it makes the appropriate sound.*)

THELMA: A hundred and forty-nine.

(*She hands the iron's plug up to* HARRIS *and
accepts from him the warm bulb.*)

HARRIS: I never took semaphor as a sophomore, morse
the pity.

(THELMA *looks at him icily but he has his own
cool.*) I used the time in a vain attempt to get the
Rockefeller girl to marry me for my sense of
humour. Would you pass my hat?

(THELMA *passes him the bowler hat, which he
puts on his head. He then inserts the iron plug
into the light socket, deftly removing his hat and
hanging it on a banana, thus cancelling out the
imbalance threatened by the weight of the plug
and its flex.* THELMA's *attention does not stay to
be impressed.*)

THELMA: For some reason, my mind keeps returning to
that one-legged footballer we passed in the car.
. . . What *position* do you suppose he plays?

(HARRIS *has got down off the chair and looked*
critically around.)

HARRIS: Bit dark in here.

(*The natural light from the window is indeed*
somewhat inadequate. THELMA *pursues her own*
thoughts and a path to the light switch,
positioned by the door at Stage L, *which controls*
the ceiling light, or, at the moment, the iron.)

THELMA: I keep thinking about him. What guts he must
have!

HARRIS: Put the light on.

(THELMA *independently depresses the light switch,*
and the red warm-up light on the iron comes on.
HARRIS *regards it sceptically.*)

Most unsatisfactory.

THELMA: I mean, what fantastic *pluck*! What real never-
say-die *spirit*, you know what I mean? (*Pause.*)
Bloody unfair on the rest of the team, mind you
—you'd think the decent thing would have been
to hang up his boot. *What are you doing now?!*
(*For* HARRIS *has gone upstage to the table lamp*
resting amid the barricade and tried, without
result, to turn it on, whereupon he has started to
blow violently against the shade. He replies
immediately.)

HARRIS: Filthy. Hasn't been dusted for weeks. I could
write my name on it.

(*He proceeds to do so, in full, remarking the*
while:)

It wasn't a football, it was a turtle.

THELMA: A turtle?

HARRIS: Or a large tortoise.

THELMA: *What?*

HARRIS: He was carrying a tortoise.

THELMA: You must be blind.

HARRIS: (*equably*) It was he who was blind. What happened to the bulb?

(*He means the bulb from the table lamp.*
THELMA however, holds out the warm bulb.)

THELMA: Here.

HARRIS: What did you take the bulb out for?

THELMA: No, that was the one you put in the bathroom. *This* is the one which——

(*As he takes the bulb from her by the metal end and flips it angrily into the air, catching it by the glass.*)

——you just took out——

HARRIS: (*shouts*) Not by the metal end!

(*Irritably he goes to insert the bulb into the table lamp.*)

THELMA: And how do you explain the West Bromwich Albion football shirt?

HARRIS: Pyjamas—he was wearing pyjamas.

(*He successfully switches on the lamp, raising the gloom considerably as he gazes moodily around. He continues to speak, characteristically, without punctuation.*)

This place is run like a madhouse. What's that

policeman staring at?

(THELMA *turns to the window, marches up to it and viciously draws the curtains together.*)

THELMA: Bloody nerve!

(*There is a piercing scream, from* MOTHER *as she jerks her foot away from the heated-up iron. This causes some confusion and cries of pain from* MOTHER *and cries of "Mother!" from* THELMA *who snatches up the iron and places it on the wooden chair, the fruit adjusting itself accordingly.* MOTHER *is now sitting up on the ironing board, facing the audience, her burned foot clutched in her lap, the other hanging down. Her first audible word seems to be a vulgarity; but is not.*)

MOTHER: *Butter!*

THELMA: (*primly*) Now there's no need to use language——

MOTHER: Get some butter!

THELMA: *Butter!*—Get butter, Reginald!

(HARRIS *rushes out.* THELMA *grabs the phone.*)

(*Dialling.*) Don't move—whatever you do don't move—Hello!—I want an ambulance!

(*There is a loud knocking on the door.* THELMA *drops the phone* (*it falls into the cradle*) *and rushes to the window, shouting.*)

Who is it?

(*She draws back the curtains, and the Policeman reappears.*)

HOLMES: It's the police!

THELMA: (*furiously*) I asked for an ambulance!

(*She viciously draws the curtains together and dashes back to pick up the phone.*)

(HARRIS *rushes in with half a pound of soft butter on a butter dish.*)

HARRIS: Where do you want it, mother?

MOTHER: On my foot, you nincompoop.

(HARRIS *slams the butter up against the sole of* MOTHER'*s undamaged foot.*)

(*The confusion ceases at once.* THELMA *replaces the phone and stands quietly.* HARRIS *stands up looking slightly crestfallen.* MOTHER *regards him glacially. There is a silence.*)

You married a fool, Thelma.

(MOTHER *gets down on the floor, on her good, though buttered, foot.*)

Has the bathroom light been repaired?

HARRIS: I put in a new bulb, mother.

MOTHER: I hope you cleaned your boots.

(MOTHER *hops one-legged across the stage to the door and leaves, not before delivering the following threat.*)

I shall be back for my practice.

(*Certain things are integrated with the following dialogue.*)

(*The iron goes back on the ironing board. The fruit adjusts.*)

(THELMA *irons the white dress shirt while* HARRIS,

sitting on the wooden chair, takes off his waders,
which have been concealing not only his trousers
but his black patent leather shoes. HARRIS *crams*
the waders into the cupboard in the barricade of
furniture.)

(*When the shirt has been ironed,* HARRIS *puts it*
on, and puts on the bow-tie, and finally the coat.
After ironing, HARRIS *climbs back on the wooden*
chair to remove the iron plug and, of course, the
bowler hat, which, for want of anywhere else, he
puts on his head.)

(MOTHER *leaves the room.*)

HARRIS: Don't start blaming me. She could have lain on the floor.

THELMA: Oh yes—very nice—with my back in the state it's in—you'd rather I bent double.

HARRIS: You could have squatted over her. It's not *my* fault that the furniture could not be put to its proper use in its proper place.

THELMA: *If* you're referring to the Cricklewood Lyceum——

HARRIS: I *am* referring to the Cricklewood Lyceum—it was a fiasco——

THELMA: You know perfectly well that my foot got caught in my hem——

HARRIS: With *your* legs?—your feet don't *reach* your hem.

THELMA: My legs are insured for £5,000!

HARRIS: Only against theft. The fact of the matter is, it

was a botch from first to last, and that is why we find ourselves having to go through it again at the eleventh hour, half of which has now gone. *We are never going to get away on time!*

THELMA: (*ironing the shirt*) I am being as quick as I can. All I can say is I'll be glad when it's all over and things are back to normal. It's making you short-tempered and argumentative. You contradict everything I say——

HARRIS: (*heatedly*) *That* I deny——

THELMA: I've only got to mention that the footballer had a football under his arm and you start insisting it was a tortoise. Why a footballer should play with a tortoise is a question which you don't seem prepared to face.

HARRIS: (*calmingly, reasonably*) Look—he was not a footballer. He was just a chap in striped pyjamas. It was a perfectly natural, not to say uninteresting, mistake and it led you to the further and even more boring misapprehension that what he was carrying was a football—whereas *I*——

THELMA: Whereas you, accepting as a matter of course a pyjama-clad figure in the street, leap to the natural conclusion that he must be carrying a tortoise.

HARRIS: The man obviously had his reasons.

THELMA: You've got to admit that a football is more likely.

HARRIS: More likely?

THELMA: In the sense that there would be more footballs than tortoises in a built-up area.

HARRIS: Leaving aside the fact that your premise is far from self-evident, it is more *likely*, by that criterion, that what the fellow had under his arm was a Christmas pudding or a copy of Whitaker's Almanac, but I happened to see him with my own eyes——

THELMA: We all saw him——

HARRIS: —and he was an old man with one leg and a white beard, dressed in pyjamas, hopping along in the rain with a tortoise under his arm and brandishing a white stick to clear a path through those gifted with sight——

THELMA: There was no one else on the pavement.

HARRIS: Since he was blind he could hardly be expected to know that.

THELMA: Who said he was blind? *You* say so——

HARRIS: (*heatedly*) He had a white stick, woman!

THELMA: (*equably*) In my opinion it was an ivory cane.

HARRIS: (*shouting*) An ivory cane IS a white stick!!
(*This seems to exhaust them both.* THELMA *irons placidly, though still rebellious. After a while....*)

THELMA: (*scornfully*) Pyjamas . . . I suppose he was hopping in his sleep. Yes, I can see it now—a bad dream—he leaps to his foot, grabs his tortoise and feels his way into the street——

HARRIS: I am only telling you what I saw! And I suggest

to you that a blind one-legged white-bearded footballer would have a hard time keeping his place in West Bromwich Albion

THELMA: He was a young chap.

HARRIS: (*patiently*) He had a white beard.

THELMA: Shaving foam.

HARRIS: (*leaping up*) Have you taken leave of your senses?

THELMA: (*strongly*) It was shaving foam! In pyjamas, if you insist, striped in the colours of West Bromwich Albion, if you allow, carrying under his arm, if not a football then something very similar like a wineskin or a pair of bagpipes, and swinging a white stick in the form of an ivory cane——

HARRIS: Bagpipes?

THELMA: —*but what he had on his face was definitely shaving foam!* (*Pause.*) Or possibly some kind of yashmak.

(HARRIS *is almost speechless.*)

HARRIS: The most—*the very most*—I am prepared to concede is that he *may* have been a sort of street arab making off with his lute—*but young he was not and white-bearded he was!*

THELMA: His *loot*?

HARRIS: (*expansively*) Or his mandolin—Who's to say?

THELMA: You admit he could have been musical?

HARRIS: I admit nothing of the sort! As a matter of fact, if he had been an Arab musician, the likelihood is that he would have been carrying a gourd—

which is very much the shape and size of a tortoise, which strongly suggests that I was right in my initial conjecture: white beard, white stick, pyjamas, tortoise. I refuse to discuss it any further.

THELMA: You'll never admit you're wrong, will you?

HARRIS: On the contrary, if I were ever wrong I would be the *first* to admit it. But these outlandish embellishments of yours are gratuitous and strain the credulity.

THELMA: (*sighing*) We should have stopped and taken a photograph. Then we wouldn't be having these arguments.

HARRIS: (*morosely*) We wouldn't be having them if we'd stayed at home, as I myself wished to do.

THELMA: It was for mother's benefit, not yours. She doesn't often ask to be taken anywhere, and it didn't cost you much to let her have her pleasure.

HARRIS: It cost me ten shillings in parking tickets alone.

THELMA: It was only one ticket, and it was your own fault for not putting any money in the meter. The truth is that we are very fortunate that a woman of her age still has an active interest, even if it is the tuba.

HARRIS: Active interest?—she's an obsessed woman; dragging us half way across London—you'd think having one in the house and playing it morning, noon and night would be enough for anyone. It's certainly too much for me.

THELMA: She's entitled to practise, just as much as we are.

HARRIS: But it's our house.

THELMA: You shouldn't have asked her to move in if you felt like that.

HARRIS: It was your idea.

THELMA: You agreed to it.

HARRIS: I agreed to her living out her last days among her loved ones—I said nothing about having her underfoot for half a lifetime.

THELMA: You said it would be useful for baby-sitting.

HARRIS: We haven't got any *children*!

THELMA: That's hardly her fault. (*Pause.*) Or mine.
(HARRIS *gets slowly to his feet.*)

HARRIS: How dare you? How *dare* you! Right—that's it! I've put up with a lot of slanders but my indulgence is now at an end. This is my house and you can tell your mother to pack her tuba and get out!

THELMA: But, Reginald——

HARRIS: No—you have pushed me too far. When I married you I didn't expect to have your mother——

THELMA: (*shouting back at him*) She's not my mother— she's *your* mother!

HARRIS: (*immediately*) *Rubbish!*
(*However, he sits down rather suddenly.*)
(*calmer*) My mother is a . . . tall . . . aristocratic

woman, in a red mac . . . answers to the name of . . .

THELMA: That's your Aunt——

THELMA:⎱
HARRIS:⎰ —Jessica.

(HARRIS *stands up and sits down immediately. His manner is agitated. He is by now fully dressed.*)
(THELMA *folds the ironing board and takes it out of the room.*)
(MOTHER *enters, from her bath, robed or dressed, without the bathing cap, but still hopping on one foot. She hops across the room.*)

MOTHER: The bulb in the bathroom's gone again.

(*She leaves by the other door.* HARRIS *gets up and goes to the cupboard, extracting his waders.*
MOTHER *returns, hopping, carrying a large felt bag.*)

I let the water out.

(HARRIS *stuffs the waders back into the cupboard. He moves towards the door, but is most unsettled. He halts, turns and addresses his* MOTHER, *who is now on the wooden chair.*)

HARRIS: (*rather aggressively*) Would you like a cup of tea, Mum?

(*The old lady is startled by the appellation. She looks up, straight ahead, then turns to look at* HARRIS *in a resentful manner.* HARRIS *quails. He turns and is about to leave again when there is a loud knocking on the street door.*)

(MOTHER continues fiddling with the felt bag, from which, at this moment she withdraws her tuba. HARRIS with the air of a man more kicked against than kicking, approaches the pile of furniture and begins to take it apart as MOTHER puts the tuba to her lips.)

(MOTHER plays while HARRIS moves the furniture piece by piece into its proper place. Before he has finished, THELMA enters with a drink in one hand and a flower vase in the other. She puts them down and helps HARRIS with the heavier pieces.)

(The long, low table is placed centrally under the lampshade. The settee goes behind it and a comfortable chair goes either side. This is managed so that MOTHER does not have to move from her position on the wooden chair, or desist from playing her jaunty tune, until the last stages, just before the police enter. When they do so (INSPECTOR FOOT and PC HOLMES), everything is in place, the wooden chair put back against the wall, and the three people seated comfortably. THELMA smoking and holding her drink; the tuba out of view, perhaps behind MOTHER's chair.)

(The only surviving oddity is the fruit basket, when the door is finally flung open and FOOT charges into the room, right downstage, with HOLMES taking up position in a downstage corner and naturally looking a little taken aback.)

FOOT: What is the meaning of this bizarre spectacle?!!

(*Pause. They all squint about.*)

THELMA: The counterweight fell down and broke. Is that a crime?

(FOOT *clasps both hands behind his back and goes into an aggressive playing-for-time stroll, passing* HOLMES.)

(FOOT *speaks out of the corner of his mouth.*)

FOOT: Got the right house, have you?

HOLMES: Yes, sir.

(FOOT *continues his stroll.* HARRIS *would like to help.*)

MOTHER: (*uncertainly*) Is it all right for me to practice?

(FOOT *ignores her, his eyes darting desperately about until they fix on the table-lamp.* FOOT *stops dead. His head moves slightly, along the line of the lampshade reading the words scrawled on it.*)

FOOT: (*trimphantly*) Reginald William Harris?

HARRIS: Thirty-seven Mafeking Villas.

FOOT: You are addressing a police officer not an envelope. Would you kindly answer my questions in the right order.

HARRIS: I'm sorry.

(FOOT *turns his back on* HARRIS, *denoting a fresh start, and barks.*)

FOOT: Reginald William Harris!

HARRIS: Here.

FOOT: Where do you live?—*you're doing it again!!!*

MOTHER: Who is that man?

FOOT: I am Chief Inspector Foot.

(HARRIS *rises to his feet with a broad enchanted smile.*)

HARRIS: Not Foot of the Y——

FOOT: (*screams*) *Silence!*

(FOOT *starts travelling again, keeping his agitation almost under control, ignoring* MOTHER's *murmur.*)

MOTHER: Can I practice now?

(FOOT *arrives at* HOLMES, *and addresses him out of the corner of his mouth.*)

FOOT: Quite sure? You never mentioned the fruit.

HOLMES: (*plaintively*) There was so much else. . . .

FOOT: Better have a look round.

HOLMES: Yes, sir.

(THELMA *ignores the convention of the "aside", raising her voice and her head.*)

THELMA: I'm afraid things are a bit of a mess.

FOOT: (*briskly*) I can't help that. You know what they say—clean knickers every day, you never know when you might be run over. Well it's happened to you on a big scale.

(HARRIS *regains his feet.*)

HARRIS: Just a minute. Have you got a search warrant?

(HOLMES *pauses.*)

FOOT: Yes.

HARRIS: Can I see it?

FOOT: I can't put my hand to it at the moment.

HARRIS: (*incredulous*) You can't *find* your search warrant!

FOOT: (*smoothly*) I had it about my person when I came in. I may have dropped it. Have a look round, Holmes.

(THELMA *rises to her feet with a broad enchanted smile.*)

THELMA: *Not——*

FOOT: (*screams*) *Be quiet!*

(THELMA *sits down.* HARRIS *will not.*)

HARRIS: Now look here——

FOOT: Can I see your television licence?

(HARRIS *freezes with his mouth open. After a long moment he closes it.*)

HARRIS: (*vaguely*) Er, it must be about . . . somewhere . . .

FOOT: Good. While you're looking for your television licence, Holmes will look for the search warrant.

(HARRIS *sits down thoughtfully.*)

(*To* HOLMES.) It could have blown about a bit or slipped down under the floorboards.

HOLMES: Right, sir.

(HOLMES *begins to crawl around the room.*)

MOTHER: Is it all right for me to practice?

(FOOT *ignores her. He stands looking down smugly at* HARRIS.)

FOOT: Yes, I expect you're wondering what gave you away.

HARRIS: (*wanly*) Was it one of those detector vans?

(*But* FOOT *is already on the move.*)

FOOT: Well, I'll tell you. It's a simple tale—no hot tips from Interpol, no days and nights of keeping watch in the rain, no trouser turn-ups hoovered by Forensics or undercover agents selling the *Evening News* in Chinatown—no!—just a plain ordinary copper on his beat! Yes! —the PC is still the best tool the Yard has got!——

(HOLMES *is behind him, on his hands and knees.*)

HOLMES: Excuse me, sir.

FOOT: (*irritated*) Not in here; *around.*

HOLMES: (*getting to his feet*) Yes, sir. Is this anything, sir?

(*He hands* FOOT *a .22 lead slug which he has found on the floor.* FOOT *accepts it unheedingly; he is already talking.* HOLMES *leaves the room.*)

FOOT: He's not one of your TV heroes, young Holmes—he's just a young man doing his job and doing it well—sometimes not seeing his kids—Dean, five, and Sharon, three—for days on end—often getting home after his wife's asleep and back on the beat before she wakes— tireless, methodical, eagle-eyed—always ready with a friendly word for the old lag crossing the road or sixpence for the old lady trying to go straight——

(HOLMES *has re-entered the room and has been dogging* FOOT'*s footsteps, waiting for an opportunity to speak, which he now deduces, wrongly, has presented itself.*)

HOLMES: To tell you the truth, sir, I'm not absolutely
sure what a search warrant looks like. . . .
(*But* FOOT *marches on, round the right-angle of
the room, while* HOLMES *plods stolidly on and out
without changing course. As* FOOT *moves he is
weighing and jiggling in his hand the lead slug,
and he has been becoming more aware of its
presence there.*)

FOOT: Yes, that's the sort of metal that has brought
you to book.
(FOOT *absently examines the object in his hand.
He seems surprised at finding it there.*)
When Holmes got back to the station and
described to me the scene he had witnessed
through your window, I realized he had
stumbled on something even bigger than
even. . . .
(*He tails off, and whirls on them, holding up the
metal slug.*)
Do any of you know what this is?
(THELMA *holds up her hand.*)
Well?
(THELMA *gets up and takes the slug out of* FOOT's
hand.)

THELMA: It's a lead slug from a .22 calibre pistol. Thank
you.
(*She tosses the slug into the metal bin wherein
it makes the appropriate sound.*)

A hundred and fifty.

(*She returns to her seat.* FOOT *walks over to the metal bin and peers into it. He bends and takes out a handful of lead slugs and lets them fall back. He stoops again and comes up with the broken halves of the porcelain container that had held the slugs and acted as the counterweight to the light fitting. He regards the basket of fruit. He drops the debris back into the bin. He addresses himself to* THELMA.)

FOOT: It is my duty to tell you that I am not satisfied with your reply.

THELMA: What was the question?

FOOT: That is hardly the point.

THELMA: Ask me another.

FOOT: Very well. Why did it take you so long to answer the door?

THELMA: The furniture was piled up against it.

FOOT: (*sneeringly*) Really? Expecting visitors, Mrs. Harris?

THELMA: On the contrary.

FOOT: In my experience your conduct usually indicates that visitors are expected.

THELMA: I am prepared to defend myself against any logician you care to produce.

FOOT: (*snaps*) Do you often stack the furniture up against the door?

THELMA: Yes. Is that a crime?

FOOT: (*furiously*) Will you stop trying to exploit my

professional knowledge for your private ends!—
I didn't do twenty years of hard grind to have
my brains picked by every ignorant layman who
finds out I'm a copper!

(HARRIS *has relapsed into a private brood, from
which this outburst rouses him. He has decided
to capitulate. He stands up.*)

HARRIS: All right! Can we call off this game of cat and
mouse?! I haven't *got* a television licence—I
kept meaning to get one but somehow. . . .

(FOOT *turns to him.*)

FOOT: Then perhaps you have a diploma from the
Royal College of Surgeons.

HARRIS: (*taken aback*) I'm afraid not. I didn't realize
they were compulsory.

FOOT: (*without punctuation*) I have reason to believe
that within the last hour in this room you
performed without anaesthetic an illegal
operation on a bald nigger minstrel about
five-foot-two or Pakistani and that is only the
beginning!

HARRIS: I deny it!

FOOT: Furthermore, that this is a disorderly house!

HARRIS: *That* I admit—Thelma, I've said it before and
I'll say it again——

THELMA: (*shouting angrily*) Don't you come that with me!
—what with the dancing, the travelling, ironing
your shirts, massaging your mother and starting
all over every morning, I haven't got time to

wipe my nose!

HARRIS: (*equally roused*) *That's* what I want to talk to
you about—sniff-sniff—it's a disgusting habit
in a woman——

THELMA: (*shouting*) All right—so I've got a cold!—
(*Turning to the world, which happens to be in the
direction of* FOOT)—Is that a crime?

FOOT: (*hysterically*) I will not warn you again!
(*He patrols furiously.*)
The disorderliness I was referring to consists of
immoral conduct—tarted-up harpies staggering
about drunk to the wide, naked men in rubber
garments hanging from the lampshade—Have
you got a music licence? (*As he passes the
gramophone.*)

HARRIS: There is obviously a perfectly logical reason for
everything.

FOOT: There is, and I mean to make it stick! What
was the nature of this operation?
(FOOT *finds himself staring at a line of single
greasy footprints leading across the room. He
hops along the trail, fascinated, until he reaches
the door to* MOTHER's *bath. He turns.*)
(*Quietly.*) The D.P.P. is going to take a very
poor view if you have been offering cut-price
amputations to immigrants.
(HOLMES *enters excitedly with the ironing board.*)

HOLMES: Sir!

FOOT: That's an ironing board.

HOLMES: (*instantaneously demoralized*) Yes, sir.

FOOT: What we're looking for is a darkie short of a leg or two.

HOLMES: (*retiring*) Right, sir.

MOTHER: Is it all right for me to practice?

FOOT: No, it is not all right! Ministry standards may be lax but we draw the line at Home Surgery to bring in the little luxuries of life.

MOTHER: I only practice on the tuba.

FOOT: Tuba, femur, fibula—it takes more than a penchant for rubber gloves to get a licence nowadays.

MOTHER: The man's quite mad.

FOOT: That's what they said at the station when I sent young Holmes to take a turn down Mafeking Villas, but everything I have heard about events here today convinces me that you are up to your neck in the Crippled Minstrel Caper!

THELMA: Is that a dance?

HARRIS: My wife and I are always on the look-out for novelty numbers. We're prepared to go out on a limb if it's not in bad taste.

FOOT: (*shouting him down*) Will you kindly stop interrupting while I am about to embark on my exegesis!! (*Pauses, he collects himself.*) The story begins about lunchtime today. The facts appear to be that shortly after two o'clock this afternoon, the talented though handicapped doyen of the Victoria Palace Happy Minstrel Troupe emerged from his dressing-room in blackface, and entered the sanctum of the box-office staff; whereupon, having broken his crutch over the heads of those good ladies, the intrepid uniped made off with the advance takings stuffed into the crocodile boot which, it goes without saying, he had surplus to his conventional requirements.

HARRIS: It must have been a unique moment in the annals of crime.

FOOT: Admittedly, the scene as I have described it is as yet my own reconstruction based on an eye-witness account of the man's flight down nearby Ponsonby Place, where, it is my firm conjecture, Harris, he was driven off by accomplices in a fast car. They might have got away with it had it not been for an elderly lady residing at number seven, who, having nothing to do but sit by her window and watch the world go by, saw flash by in front of her eyes a bizarre and desperate figure. Being herself an old devotee of minstrel shows she recognized him at once for what he was. She was even able to glimpse his broken crutch, the sort of detail that speaks volumes to an experienced detective. By the time she had made her way to her front door, the street was deserted, save for one or two tell-tale coins on the pavement. Nevertheless, it was her report which enabled me to reconstruct the sequence of events—though I am now inclined to modify the details inasmuch as the culprit may have been a genuine coloured man impersonating a minstrel in order to insinuate himself into the side door to the box office. These are just the broad strokes. My best man, Sergeant Potter, is at this moment checking the Victoria Palace end of the case and I am confidently expecting verification by telephone of my hypothesis. In any event I think you now understand why I am here.

HARRIS: No, I'm afraid I'm completely at a loss.

FOOT: Then perhaps you can explain what your car was doing in Ponsonby Place at twenty-five minutes past two this afternoon.

HARRIS: So that's it.

FOOT: Exactly. It was bad luck getting that parking ticket, Harris—one of those twists of fate that have cracked many an alibi. We traced your car and sent Constable Holmes to take a look at you.

HARRIS: But we know nothing of this outrage.

FOOT: What were you doing there, right across London?

HARRIS: We went to see an exhibition of surrealistic art at the Tate Gallery.

FOOT: I must say that in a lifetime of off-the-cuff alibis I have seldom been moved closer to open derision.

THELMA: Perhaps it would help to explain that my mother-in-law is a devotee of Maigret.

MOTHER: *Magritte.*

FOOT: I'm afraid I don't follow your drift.

HARRIS: You will when I tell you that she is an accomplished performer on, and passionate admirer in all its aspects, of the tuba.

FOOT: Tuba? (*Angrily.*) You are stretching my patience and my credulity to breaking poi—— (*He sees* MOTHER *with the tuba now on her lap.*)

MOTHER: Can I have a go now?

HARRIS: Hearing that among the canvasses on view were several depicting the instrument of her chief and indeed obsessional interest, my wife's mother, in law, or rather my mother, prevailed upon us to take her to the exhibition, which we did, notwithstanding the fact that we could ill afford the time from rehearsing for a professional engagement at the North Circular Dancerama tonight, and to which, I may say, we will shortly have to absent ourselves. (*To* THELMA *without pause.*) Have you taken up your hem?

(THELMA *gasps with dismay and self-reproach and immediately whips off her dress. This leaves her in bra and panties. Her action, since it is not especially remarkable, is not especially remarked upon.* THELMA'*s preoccupation now is to find needle and thread, in which she succeeds quite*

*quickly without leaving the room. However, her
chief problem during the ensuing minutes is her
lack of a tailor's dummy. She tries draping the
dress over various bits of furniture, and tackling
the hem, but for one reason or another—the
inadequate lighting or the lowness of the chairs,
etc.—she is intermittently frustrated until, quite
naturally and smoothly, she drapes the dress over*
HARRIS, *who simply takes no notice; indeed*
THELMA *is reduced to following him on her hands
and knees between stitches, and occasionally
asking him to keep still. Needless to say, the
dress must be sleeveless and full.)*
(There has been no pause in the dialogue.)
Look at her!—with an organized partner I
could have reached the top!

FOOT: About your alibi——

MOTHER: It was rubbish.

FOOT: Hah!

(He turns to her.)

MOTHER: Tubas on fire, tubas stuck to lions and naked
women, tubas hanging in the sky—there was one
woman with a tuba with a sack over her head
as far as I could make out. I doubt he'd ever
tried to play one; in fact if you ask me the
man must have been some kind of lunatic.

HARRIS: As my mother says, the visit was a disappoint-
ment.

THELMA: I must say I have to agree. I don't like to speak

slightingly of another artiste, but it just wasn't
life-like—I'm not saying it wasn't *good*—well
painted—but not from life, you know?

FOOT: That has no bearing on the case. Did you see
anybody you knew at the exhibition?

MOTHER: I saw Sir Adrian Boult.

FOOT: Would he be prepared to come forward?

HARRIS: You'll have to forgive the old lady. She sees Sir
Adrian Boult everywhere.

MOTHER: I saw him in Selfridges.

FOOT: Yes, quite——

MOTHER: He was buying a cushion-cover.

FOOT: (*loudly*) Can we please keep to the point! Which
happens to be that after Magritte you
apparently returned to your car parked in
Ponsonby Place, and drove off at the very
moment and from the very spot where the
escaping minstrel was last observed, which
suggests to me that you may have kept a
rendezvous and driven off with him in your car.

HARRIS: That is a monstrous allegation, and, it so
happens, a lie.

FOOT: Was there any independent witness who can
vouch for that?

MOTHER: Yes—there was that man. He waved at me
when we were driving off.

FOOT: Can you describe him?

MOTHER: Yes. He was playing hopscotch on the corner, a
man in the loose-fitting striped gaberdine of a

convicted felon. He carried a handbag under one arm, and with the other he waved at me with a cricket bat.

(FOOT *reels*.)

FOOT: Would you know him again?

MOTHER: I doubt it. He was wearing dark glasses, and a surgical mask.

(HARRIS *comes forward to restore sanity*.)

HARRIS: My mother is a bit confused, Inspector. It was a tortoise under his arm and he wasn't so much playing hopscotch as one-legged.

THELMA: (*deftly slipping the dress over* HARRIS) A tortoise or a football—he was a young man in a football shirt——

HARRIS: *If* I might just stick my oar in here, he could hardly have been a young man since he had a full white beard, and, if I'm not mistaken, side-whiskers.

THELMA: I don't wish to make an issue of this point, but since it has been raised, the energetic if spasmodic hopping of the man's movements hardly suggest someone in his dotage——

HARRIS: I saw him distinctly through the windscreen——

THELMA: It was, of course, raining at the time——

HARRIS: My windscreen wipers were in order, and working——

FOOT: At any rate, regardless of his age, convictions or hobbies, you claim that this man saw you drive off from Ponsonby Place at 2.25 this afternoon?

HARRIS: I'm afraid not, Inspector. He was blind, sweeping a path before him with a white stick——

THELMA: —a West Bromwich Albion squad member, swinging an ivory cane—for goodness sake keep still, Reginald—and get up on the table a minute, my back's breaking——
(HARRIS *mounts the low table, thus easing the angle of* THELMA'*s back.*)

HARRIS: My wife is a bit confused——

FOOT: So the best witness you can come up with is a blind, white-bearded, one-legged footballer with a tortoise. How do you account for the animal? Was it a seeing-eye tortoise?

HARRIS: I don't see that the tortoise as such requires explanation. Since the fellow was blind he needn't necessarily have known it was a tortoise. He might have picked it up in mistake for some other object such as a lute.

FOOT: His loot?

HARRIS: Or mandolin.

MOTHER: It was, in fact, an alligator handbag.

FOOT: I'm afraid I can't accept these picturesque fantasies. My wife has an alligator handbag and I defy anyone to mistake it for a musical instrument.

THELMA: *STOP!* Don't move!
(*They desist.*)
I've dropped the needle.

HARRIS: (*looking at his watch*) For God's sake,
Thelma——
THELMA: Help me find it.
(MOTHER *and* FOOT *dutifully get down on their
hands and knees with* THELMA. HARRIS *remains
standing on the table.* MOTHER *and* FOOT *are
head-to-head.*)
MOTHER: Inspector, if the man we saw was blind, who
was the other witness?
FOOT: What other witness?
MOTHER: The one who must have told the police about
our car being there.
FOOT: My dear lady, you have put your finger on one
of the ironies of this extraordinary case. I
myself live at number four Ponsonby Place,
and it was I, glancing out of an upstairs
window, who saw your car pulling away from
the kerb.
MOTHER: And yet, you never saw the minstrel?
FOOT: No, the first I knew about it was when I got to
the station late this afternoon and read the
eye-witness report sent in by the old lady. I
must have missed him by seconds, which led
me to suspect that he had driven off in your
car. I remembered seeing a yellow parking
ticket stuck in your windscreen, and the rest
was child's play.
(*The telephone rings.*)
(*Getting up and going to it.*) Ah—that will be

Sergeant Potter. We shall soon see how my
deductions tally with the facts.

(FOOT *picks up the phone. The needle search*
continues. HARRIS *stands, patient and gowned, on*
the table.)

THELMA: Can we have the top light on?

HARRIS: There's no bulb.

THELMA: Get the bulb from the bathroom.

HARRIS: It's gone again.

THELMA: Well, get any bulb!—quickly!

(MOTHER *gets to her one good foot as* FOOT
replaces the phone dumbstruck and shaken. The
table-lamp is next to the phone.)

MOTHER: Could you get the bulb out of that lamp,
Inspector?

(FOOT *looks at her unseeingly.*)

The bulb.

(FOOT, *as in a dream, turns to the bulb. His*
brain has seized up.)

You'll need a hanky or a glove.

(FOOT *ineffectually pats his pocket.*)

A woollen sock would do.

(FOOT *sits down wearily and slips off one of his*
shoes and his sock.)

HARRIS: Is something the matter with your foot, Foot?
Inspector, Foot?

(FOOT *thrusts one hand into the woollen sock.*
With the other he produces from his pocket a
pair of heavy dark glasses which he puts on.)

100

You wish to inspect your foot, Inspector?

THELMA: *Can we please have some light?*

FOOT: (*quietly*) Yes—of course—forgive me—I get this awful migraine behind the eyes—it's the shock——

MOTHER: What happened, Inspector?

FOOT: It appears that no robbery of the kind I deduced has in fact taken place among the Victoria Palace Happy Minstrel Troupe. Moreover, there is no minstrel troupe, happy or miserable, playing at that theatre or any other. My reconstruction has proved false in every particular, and it is undoubtedly being voiced back at the station that my past success at deductions of a penetrating character has caused me finally to overreach myself in circumstances that could hardly be more humiliating.

(*They all sense the enormity of it.* HARRIS, *however, is unforgiving. He steps down off the table.*)

THELMA: Oh . . . I'm sorry. Is there anything we can do?

MOTHER: I've always found that bananas are very good for headaches.

HARRIS: (*nastily*) So the crime to which you have accused us of being accessories never in fact took place!

FOOT: That is the position, but before you start congratulating yourself, you still have to explain the incredible and suggestive behaviour witnessed by Constable Holmes through your window.

HARRIS: The activities in this room today have broadly speaking been of a mundane and domestic nature bordering on cliché. Police Constable Holmes obviously has an imagination as fervid and treacherous as your own. If he's found a shred of evidence to back it up then get him in here and let's see it.

FOOT: Very well! (*Calls.*) Holmes!

THELMA: Inspector, the bulb, we need the bulb.

(MOTHER *hops over to the wooden chair by the wall, in order to pick it up, though we do not see her do that.* FOOT's *attention is still on* HARRIS.)

FOOT: But bear in mind that my error was merely one of interpretation, and whatever did happen in Ponsonby Place this afternoon, your story contains a simple but revealing mistake which clearly indicates that your so-called alibi is a tissue of lies.

HARRIS: What do you mean?

FOOT: You claimed that your witness was a blind one-legged musician.

HARRIS: Roughly speaking.

FOOT: You are obviously unaware that a blind man *cannot stand on one leg*!

HARRIS: Rubbish!

FOOT: It is impossible to keep one's sense of balance

for more than a few seconds, and if you don't
believe me, try it!

(*Black-out as* FOOT *extracts the bulb.*)

HARRIS: I will!

MOTHER: Over here, Inspector.

(*In the darkness, which for these few seconds
should be total,* HARRIS *begins to count, slowly
and quietly to himself. But it is* FOOT'*s voice that
must be isolated.*)

FOOT: The sudden silence as I enter the canteen will be
more than I can bear. . . .

MOTHER: Here we are.

FOOT: The worst of it is, if I'd been up a few minutes
earlier I could have cracked the case and made
the arrest before the station even knew about it.

MOTHER: I'll need the sock.

FOOT: I'd been out with the boys from C Division till
dawn, and left my car outside the house,
thinking that I'd move it to a parking meter
before the wardens came round—in my position
one has to set an example, you know. Well, I
woke up late and my migraine was giving me
hell and my bowels were so bad I had to stop
half way through shaving, and I never gave the
traffic warden a thought till I glanced out of the
window and saw your car pulling away from
the only parking space in the road. I flung
down my razor and rushed into the street,
pausing only to grab my wife's handbag

containing the small change and her parasol to keep off the rain——

MOTHER: You won't mind if I have my practice now, will you?

FOOT: I got pretty wet because I couldn't unfurl the damned thing, and I couldn't move fast because in my haste to pull up my pyjama trousers I put both feet into the same leg. So after hopping about a bit and nearly dropping the handbag into various puddles, I just thought to hell with it all and went back in the house. My wife claimed I'd broken her new white parasol, and when I finally got out of there I had a parking ticket. I can tell you it's just been one bitch of a day.

MOTHER: Lights!

THELMA: At last.

(The central light comes on and the effect is much brighter. The light has been turned on by HOLMES *who stands rooted in the doorway with his hand still on the switch.)*

(The row on the table reads from left to right:

((1) MOTHER, *standing on her good foot only, on the wooden chair which is placed on the table; a woollen sock on one hand; playing the tuba.)*

((2) Lightshade, slowly descending towards the table.)

((3) FOOT, *with one bare foot, sunglasses, eating banana.)*

((*4*) *Fruit basket, slowly ascending.*)
((*5*) HARRIS, *gowned, blindfolded with a cushion cover over his head, arms outstretched, on one leg, counting.*)
(THELMA, *in underwear, crawling around the table, scanning the floor and sniffing.*)
(HOLMES *recoils into paralysis.*)
FOOT: Well, Constable, I think you owe us all an explanation.
(*The lampshade descends inexorably as the music continues to play; when it touches the table-top, there is no more light.*)
(*Alternatively, the lampshade could disappear down the horn of the tuba.*)

THE END

OTHER GROVE PRESS DRAMA AND THEATER PAPERBACKS

17016-X ARDEN, JOHN / Plays: One (Serjeant Musgave's Dance, The Workhouse Donkey, Armstrong's Last Goodnight) / $4.95
17208-6 BECKETT, SAMUEL / Endgame / $2.95
17233-7 BECKETT, SAMUEL / Happy Days / $2.95
17204-3 BECKETT, SAMUEL / Waiting for Godot / $3.50
17112-8 BRECHT, BERTOLT / Galileo / $2.95
17472-0 BRECHT, BERTOLT / The Threepenny Opera / $2.45
17226-4 IONESCO, EUGENE / Rhinoceros and Other Plays (The Leader, The Future Is in Eggs, or It Takes All Sorts to Make a World) / $4.95
17016-4 MAMET, DAVID / American Buffalo / $3.95
17040-7 MAMET, DAVID / A Life in the Theatre / $6.95
17043-1 MAMET, DAVID / Sexual Perversity in Chicago and The Duck Variations / $3.95
17092-X ODETS, CLIFFORD / Six Plays (Waiting for Lefty; Awake and Sing; Golden Boy; Rocket to the Moon; Till the Day I Die; Paradise Lost) / $7.95
17001-6 ORTON, JOE / The Complete Plays (The Ruffian on the Stair, The Good and Faithful Servant, The Erpingham Camp, Funeral Games, Loot, What the Butler Saw, Entertaining Mr. Sloane) / $6.95
17251-5 PINTER, HAROLD / The Homecoming / $4.95
17885-8 PINTER, HAROLD / No Man's Land / $3.95
17539-5 POMERANCE, BERNARD / The Elephant Man / $4.25
17743-6 RATTIGAN, TERENCE / Plays: One / $5.95
17884-X STOPPARD, TOM / Travesties / $3.95
17260-4 STOPPARD, TOM / Rosencrantz and Guildenstern Are Dead / $3.95
17206-X WALEY, ARTHUR, tr. and ed. / The No Plays of Japan / $7.95

GROVE PRESS, INC., 196 West Houston St., New York, N.Y. 10014